# WHY GO
*Anywhere*
# ELSE?

# WHY GO
## *Anywhere*
# ELSE?

## HOPE *and* TRUTH *for* TODAY'

A CASE FOR JESUS CHRIST

WRITTEN WITH LOVE BY:
*Nancy Hollywood-Leamer*

XULON PRESS

Xulon Press
2301 Lucien Way #415
Maitland, FL 32751
407.339.4217
www.xulonpress.com

Unless otherwise indicated, SScripture quotations taken from the King James Version (KJV) – *public domain.*

Scripture quotations taken from the New King James Version (NKJV). Copyright © 1982 by Thomas Nelson, Inc. Used by permission. All rights reserved.

Printed in the United States of America

Paperback ISBN-13: 978-1-6628-1062-6
Ebook ISBN-13: 978-1-6628-1063-3

*In dedication to Jesus, my redeemer and the restorer of my soul, to the Spirit of God who continues to realign me; who shook me from my sleep and set upon my heart the task of writing this book, and to my heavenly Father who drew me to Himself and has carried me throughout my life.- Nancy*

*"I am the good shepherd; and I know My sheep, and I am known by My own. ... and I lay down My life for the sheep. And other sheep I have which are not of this fold; them also I must bring, and they will hear My voice; and there will be one flock and one Shepherd." (John 10:14-16)*

# -ACKNOWLEDGEMENTS-

*M*y appreciation overflows for my husband, Gregg, who with the patience of a saint loves me through everything. I am especially thankful for my sister, Sue, and her daughter, Tracie, who share in my love for the Word Of God, my excitement in watching biblical prophecy unfold, as well as my urgency to share the message of hope to a lost world. I also offer my heartfelt gratitude to these online Pastors, teachers and authors who continue to encourage, inspire and strengthen me daily, and whose love for the truth is contagious: Chad Thomas of Watchman on the Wall, Brandon Holthaus and his Prophecy Updates, Pastor of Rock Harbor Church in Bakersfield, California, Jan Markel of Olive Tree Ministries and Understanding The Times Radio, Minneapolis, Minnesota, Pastor J. D. Farag and his ABCs of salvation, Calvary Chapel, Kaneohe Hawaii, Tom Hughes, Hope For Our Times Radio and Pastor of 412 Church in San Jacinto, California, Dr. David Jeremiah, author of "The Book of Signs," and many others; founder of Turning Point Ministries and Senior Pastor of Shadow Mountain Church, El Cajon, California, Pastor Greg Laurie and his Harvest Ministries; bringing thousands to salvation through his Harvest Crusades, author of many life-changing books, of Harvest Christian Church, Riverside, California, Dr. David Reagan, of Lamb and Lion Ministries, and Christ in Prophecy, Carroll Roberson of Carroll Roberson Ministries, author of "Forty Days with the Risen Savior," and others, a wonderful singer, songwriter and evangelist in Ripley, Mississippi. I'm also very grateful for the brilliant minds of Dr. Andy Woods, President of Chafer Theological College and Pastor of Sugarland Bible Church in Texas, a gifted teacher and author of several books, including "The Middle East Meltdown: The Coming Islamic Invasion of Israel," "The Falling Away – Spiritual departure or Physical Rapture," The late, great, Dr. Chuck Missler, former businessman, engineer, author and founder of Koinonia House

vii

*Ministries, L.A. Marzulli of "Politics, Prophecy and the Supernatural" channel; award winning film maker: The Nephilim Trilogy, author and lecturer with a passion for digging up the truth through archeological work as well as in his research into supernatural phenomenon, aliens and paranormal activity. Dr. Mark Eastman and his in-depth knowledge of Cosmos and Creation/Science and the Bible, which have been brought to light through his books, videos and lectures on these subjects. A special thanks to Pastor John McArthur of Grace Community Church, Sun Valley, California, the first Christian church I attended back in 1983. I have the deepest appreciation to all of these and **so many others**, not listed here. Each bringing their own unique styles, insights, opinions, and gifts, making for meaningful debate; while their opinions may differ in various areas of interest, non-essential to salvation, their goal and desire is to rightly divide the Scriptures, as they teach the full counsel of God. Above all, each of them refusing to candy coat the truth, as they "speak the **truth in love." Last but not least, I am eternally thankful for my sister, Sue, who brought me my first bible nearly 40 years ago. I don't know where I'd be without her constant love, prayers, encouragement and support.*

# CONTENTS

"To everything there is a season,
and a time to every purpose under heaven." (Ecclesiastes 3:1)

# INTRODUCTION

S everal years ago my husband, Gregg, and I were back East on vacation with my brother and sister-in-law. We were out one afternoon enjoying the sights, driving along a beautiful, rural area of Pennsylvania, when we came across a little place along the roadside with a sign that read: "GOOD FOOD, COLD BEER, HOT CHICKS – WHY GO ANYWHERE ELSE?" We all got a kick out of the sign, and although we didn't stop in, we all agreed the advertisement offered a compelling case for many travelers. Strangely enough, as we drove along that day, the question on that funny sign made me think of my faith. Many years before that day I had placed my faith in Jesus, the Son of the living God. Although throughout those years, I never doubted the truth about Jesus, and I had never lost my faith in Him, over the years in my gradual conformity to the world, I had lost myself; I had lost sight of my true purpose, and with that, I had lost the joy that I once had. Although I was extremely happy during that time of my life, happy together with the new love of my life, I realized that there is a distinct difference between "happiness" and "joy." For the most part, happiness, as good as it may *feel* at times, is "a lot of fluff." Unlike happiness, joy has a depth and can be experienced regardless of circumstances. Since then I've made my way back from the vanity and futility of this world as described by King Solomon, back to the light of life, *which is Jesus.* Although that journey is too long a story to be made short and for another time, I'll just say that I'm thankful to be back. My faith has been restored, renewed, and refreshed, and it is stronger than ever before. And as I had so many years ago, I'm jumping for joy in my faith as I walk in His light again.

You might ask, "Of all the things to believe in, why Jesus?" My answer: "**Why go anywhere else?**" History itself offers a compelling case for Jesus. I'm no scholar and I don't claim to have all the answers to the mysteries of life or death, the universe, heaven and hell...but there's something very important that has to be considered, some things that can't be ignored. **Jesus,** unlike anyone else in the history of mankind, conquered death! No other person, prophet, philosopher, religious leader, or spiritual figure has ever done that! **Death couldn't hold Jesus.** Now, I'd say that's a pretty big deal.

With death we're reminded of the frailty of life, reminded so bluntly, like a harsh jolt, that *life is a gift*, not a guarantee. On the other hand, the devastation and sadness of death is a guarantee for everyone. Back in 1965 the popular rock group The Byrds released a hit song called "Turn, Turn, Turn" inspired by the Old Testament Book of Ecclesiastes, which states so beautifully for us the facts of life; telling us in no uncertain terms that there is a time set aside for all things in this life—all things including death. So simply and yet so eloquently written, the scripture reads: "To everything there is a season, and **a time** to every purpose under heaven" (Ecclesiastes 3:1). It goes on to tell us that the two most significant events in our lives have a **designated** time: "There is **a time** to be born and a **time** to die" (Ecclesiastes 3:2). Those are very profound words. Regarding our time to die, the New Testament further tells us, "It is **appointed** unto man **once** to die" (Hebrews 9:27), confirming yet again that we **all** have an appointment *with death itself.* There are **no exceptions**: wealthy or poor, criminal or law-abiding citizen, **no one** is excluded from death. Most people are familiar with the words from the letter written to French scientist Jean Baptiste-Leroy in 1789, where Benjamin Franklin states pragmatically, **"Nothing is certain except death and taxes."** We all accept and understand that, barring a divine intervention, the question is not *if* we will die but *when*.

Knowing the inevitability of death doesn't make our pain any less to bear when we lose someone we love. While we all realize that life is fragile, we still continue doing the best we can and living our lives to the fullest each day we are given. What else can we do but be strong and move on? In the midst of all the sadness and devastation that comes with death, there is also a source of strength, comfort, and hope, because of a promise from God. For me it's about *in whom* my faith has been placed, that brings comfort, peace, hope, and strength during times of adversity and deep sadness. My life has overflowed with both, and I wanted to share with you **the source** of my strength; I wanted to offer you some important food for thought as you continue down the path of life in your own search for truth.

The apostle Peter encourages believers to "be prepared to give an answer to everyone who asks you to give a reason for the hope that we have. But do this with gentleness and respect" (1 Peter 3:15). Although I've always had a desire to share the message of God's grace, and would pray for opportunities; several years ago, I was struck with a great sense of *urgency* to share the message like never before. It was a spiritual wake-up call that I couldn't seem to ignore. In writing this, my prayer is to answer some common questions with common sense—to bring some light into the darkness, to take a look at the various beliefs that the world has embraced, to discuss the various reasons people use for rejecting Christianity, as well as to expose the subtle deception and seduction that have crept into so many of today's churches, drawing people in, while leading them astray; and the fact that thousands of years ago it was written that this very thing would happen in the last days. I'd like to share the comfort in knowing the sovereignty of God; to bring real hope that can only be found in *truth*, to a world in chaos, as I share a glorious glimpse of future events. Most importantly I want to give an answer for my faith and offer **a compelling case for Jesus** as you consider all of your options.

As for fellow believers, my prayer is to *reignite* your faith as we look forward to the wonderful things that God has in store for us, and more so that you will be *strengthened* and *encouraged* in your faith, that you will be *realigned* in your walk and *recommitted* in *your true purpose* as we reflect on the magnificence of God and the amazing things He has already done for us. As a believer I'm also encouraged to "speak **the truth** in love" (Ephesians 4:15), which can be like a high-wire act in this day and age, but that's my mission here. **This matter of truth** may be of interest to those who are actively seeking truth as well as to those who are seeking truth and may not even be aware of it.

"Faith is the substance of things hoped for,
the evidence of things not seen." (Hebrews 11:1)

## Chapter One

## EVERYONE CAN'T BE RIGHT

**M**any theories have been argued about what's in store for us after we die. *Everyone has **faith** in something.* Even if you *believe* there is **no** God, believing that when we die, we simply cease to exist, that we've evolved from nearly nothing and our time here is nothing more than the legacy we leave behind. *That* takes faith. Others have said they believe in their own understanding of God; they have faith in a "god" custom-designed to fit their own idea of what a loving god should be or do: "My god wouldn't do this or a 'loving' god wouldn't do that . . ." in a sense, becoming the creator of their own god. Some have faith in an afterlife that involves a certain amount of faith in themselves; they have faith that if they're a "good person" they'll go to heaven, thereby setting their own standards as to what's good enough to make the cut. But depending on whether you look to the left or the right of you, you're sure to find someone who's "better" or "worse" than yourself when measuring by your own standards. So who decides who is good enough? Some place their faith in a religious system: they have faith that by belonging to a religious group or a church, following various rules and rituals, they can **earn** their way into heaven or avoid going to hell. There are those who have faith in reincarnation, believing that when they die, they will come back again and again, die many times over till they work out all the "bad karma" from one life to another and perhaps even return in one form or another. Other Eastern religions have the belief that they **are** god and only have to "realize" it through meditation. I also know those who believe that there is no distinction between the creation and the Creator, who will tell you that "everything is god . . . and god is everything"—the earth, the sun, the stars, and so on. Others believe in many gods: the sun god, the moon god, the god of this or the god of that. There are those who rely on faith in their own ability to create something, be it an event or a circumstance: they have faith in the power of their own mind, the power of positive thinking. In other words, if they have enough faith, believe it, visualize it, or meditate on it hard enough, it will come to be. Although, their faith—when carried to its logical conclusion—will bring them to the realization that there may be someone else "believing," "meditating," or "visualizing" the exact opposite of the goal or experience they're trying to achieve. Some may pick and choose particular things that appeal to them about various religions and philosophies and place their faith in those things. Many these days have an all-inclusive, non-offensive attitude about faith, believing that there are many roads, all leading to heaven. Others may simply prefer to avoid thinking too deeply or too much about the purpose of their life, or the reality of death, as they go through their days with faith that everything will turn out okay in the end. Just naming a few, you can see the wide range of beliefs—**all requiring faith**.

While it may not be popular or politically correct to say in this day and age, it also doesn't take a genius to figure out that when views oppose each other so drastically, **everyone can't be right**. For example, whether you attribute the discovery to scientist and ancient Greek astronomer Alexander Eratosthenes or Italian explorer Christopher Columbus, it is considered by most, a well-known fact that the earth is round. Prior to the discovery that the earth is round, among various beliefs, many believed the earth to be flat. My point is this: what people believe about the earth has **no effect** on the reality and **the truth** about it. In other words, **people's beliefs will not change the shape, size, or geographical landscape of the earth.**

That same principle stands true when we consider the matters of death, and the truth about it, that we will all face sooner or later. You see, unless we simply cease to exist, each of us will make our own "discovery" one day. We will discover the **reality** of eternity and the **truth** about what's in store for us after we die. Much like the discovery that the earth is round, what *we* believe or don't believe will have no effect on **the truth**, which **remains to be seen**. Contemplating all of this, I realize that without **substance** and **evidence**, faith is merely a word: it means nothing without **a solid foundation** to rest it upon.

"Everyone who is **of the truth** hears My voice." (John 18:37)

## Chapter Two

# SUBSTANCE, EVIDENCE, AND JESUS

**T**ruth is uncompromising, inflexible, and **absolute**, and will not change regardless of what *we* believe. Ultimately there is a truth about everything. Some truths we already know and some truths we have yet to know. The truth is what it is. There are some universal truths that we can all agree on. For example, the sky is blue, water is wet, grass is green, and so on. However, we may not all agree on *the truth* about what happens to us after we die. Nevertheless, it is yet another truth, and in time *that* truth will be revealed to each of us. And like I said, *everyone can't be right.* Unrevealed truth can't be proven or dis-proven and therefore requires *faith.* So it stands to reason that truth being what it is, where you place your faith today will make a world of difference once the truth is revealed. It will reveal the vast difference between devastation and joy the split second we leave this earth. Or will you simply cease to exist?

Is there a solid foundation for the various things people put their faith in? What are the foundations for these various beliefs? Are they just convenient, comforting, or nice-sounding things to believe in? Are they deceptions, diversions, distractions, or creative ways to ignore the reality or even the possibility of God? Or have people conjured up the idea of God because they want something to believe in? What is the truth? In today's world, the word *truth* has become ambiguous, with new "woke" terms such as "my truth" and "your truth" being bandied around as if they have any meaning at all. When it comes to eternity, *truth* will not be determined by *my* truth or *your* truth. Rather what will be revealed will be **the** *truth*. Each day passing brings us one day closer to death, and with our eternity at stake, today is a good time to give careful consideration to **this matter of truth**.

When the Jewish leaders brought Jesus before the Roman Governor, Pontius Pilate, for the offense of claiming to be the king of the Jews, Jesus stood at the mercy of Pilate, who asked Him what He had done. Jesus responded, "My Kingdom is **not** of this world." Pilate then asked Him, "Are you a king then?" Jesus responded, "You say **rightly** that I am a King. **For this cause** I have come into the world, **that I should bear witness to <u>the truth</u>**. Everyone who is **of the truth** hears My voice." Pilate's next question was this: **"What is truth?"** (John 18:36–38).

As you consider that question and consider all of your options, I pray that you'll consider Jesus, a historical figure who stunningly claimed to be "The Way, <u>**The Truth**</u> and The Life" (John 14:6). The things we know about Jesus have come to us in the very same way as any other historical figure that came before our time: through the written accounts of the people who knew them and the close confidants of their day. The recorded accounts of Jesus have been scrutinized by both secular and non-secular historical scholars. **Jesus** is named among the list titled: "The Most Important Figures in Ancient History" alongside Julius Caesar, Alexander the Great, Archimedes, Confucius, and so on. Among that list, and in fact among any list, Jesus is the **only** person in the history of mankind to **conquer death**. Like I said, that's a pretty big deal!

During His time with the apostles, aside from the many miracles they witnessed, the apostles, Peter, John and James were specially privileged to witness the sheer majesty of Jesus as He was transfigured before them; He was shown to them in His radiant state of heavenly glory; it was so overwhelming that they fell face down on the ground before Him. Peter tells us this: "For we did not follow cunningly devised fables when we made known to you the *power* and the coming of our Lord Jesus Christ, but we were *eyewitnesses* of His majesty. For He received from *God the Father* honor and glory when such a voice came to Him *from the Excellent Glory*: 'This is My beloved Son, in whom I am well pleased.' And we heard the voice which came down from heaven..." (2 Peter 1:16-18).

After His death, Jesus appeared first to Mary Magdalene and also to Mary the mother of James, who had gone to the borrowed tomb where His body had been laid. Shortly after, Jesus appeared before His followers in the upper room, saying, "Peace be with you." In their initial shock and amazement, Jesus extended an offer, stretching out His hands to them: "See my hands and My feet, see that it is I Myself; touch Me and see, for a spirit does not have flesh and bones as you see that I have" (Luke 24:39). You see, Jesus didn't appear to them as a nebulous, mystical phantom or floating spirit with no tangibility. Although now resurrected, He was in His *glorified body*; He was able to defy the laws of nature in various ways: appearing and vanishing before their eyes and so on. There He was with unmistakable power and majesty. Yet, He was the same flesh-and-bone man that they had known for years and had grown to love, now standing before them, displaying the marks of the wounds He endured in His own death and crucifixion, which they had all witnessed.

The disciple, Thomas, was not with the others in the upper room when Jesus made His first appearance, but he came a week or so later. It was this encounter that the often-used idiom "doubting Thomas" was derived from: When Thomas arrived, he was greeted by the others with excitement and joy, and they told him, "We've seen the Lord!" Thomas was skeptical by nature and said to them, "Unless I see the nail marks in His hands and put my finger where the nails were, and put my hand into his side, I will not believe" (John 20:25). Although the doors were locked in the upper room, Jesus appeared again before them and said,

"Peace be with you." Then Jesus turned to Thomas and said, "Put your finger here; see my hands. Reach out your hand and put it into my side. Stop doubting Thomas and believe" (John 20:27). Thomas was overwhelmed with emotion, and falling at the feet of Jesus, he cried out to Him, "My Lord and my God" (John 20:28). Then Jesus said to Thomas, "You have seen and you believe, blessed are those who have not seen, yet believe" (John 20:29). Beyond those appearances and aside from His disciples, Jesus was witnessed by more than five hundred people over the course of forty days, at various places and on at least twelve separate occasions.

Many of those who witnessed Jesus to be very much alive after His resurrection had also witnessed His brutal crucifixion and death. After His resurrection, Jesus was touched and embraced; He drank and broke bread with various groups of followers over the course of several weeks. During those final weeks, Jesus continued to preach **His message of *Salvation* and the message of *His coming Kingdom*.** The earthly mission and ministry of Jesus finally came to its spectacular end—in the midst of onlookers—at the place called the Mount of Olives, where Jesus was taken up into the clouds. It was there on the Mount of Olives that Jesus gave His disciples their final instructions before He left them.

He blessed them and He was taken up into heaven before their very eyes, as He ascended before them, a cloud began to cover Him from their sight. They were still looking intently up into the sky, when suddenly two men dressed in white, appeared beside them. Men of Galilee, why do you stand here looking into the sky? **This same Jesus**, who has been taken from you into heaven, **will come back** in the same way that you have seen Him go into heaven. Astounded at what they had just seen, they traveled back to Jerusalem with great joy. (Luke 24:51, Acts 1:9–11, Mark 16:9)

These and many other facts about **Jesus** and His miraculous resurrection are recorded in history, and in fact changed the course of history. That in itself is enough for me to **sit up and take notice**. In spite of the skeptics who have challenged the authority and authenticity of scripture, the record of this unmatched, monumental event has met all of the demands of recorded historical reliability. **Unlike** every other religious leader in history, the grave of Jesus remains empty!

**Jesus conquered the very thing that the vast majority of people spend their entire lives trying to avoid—*death*.** Without the resurrection, Jesus would be nothing more than another dead religious leader, along with all the others. Jesus's followers refused to recant their witness of Him as the Son of God and the resurrected Savior even to their own violent deaths. All any of them had to do was to deny Jesus and they could walk away, but they refused; they simply couldn't do it. The young apostle Stephen, historically considered the first martyr of Christ, said this: "Look, I see the heavens opened and I see the Son of Man, standing in His place of honor at the right hand of The Father" (Acts 7:56) as the religious leaders were about to drag him out to the street to stone him to death. In the midst of his own destruction, Stephen cried out, "'Lord Jesus, receive my spirit' and he knelt down and shouted, 'Lord, forgive them for what they have done.' Then he died" (Acts 7:59). Jesus's disciples, with the exception of John, who was banished to the island of Patmos (where He wrote the Book of Revelation) died as martyrs because they could not deny what they knew to be true. **Jesus is a *living* God and Savior.** He is sitting right now in the heavens, in full power, at the right hand of His Father until the appointed and predetermined time of His return. Jesus gave His life willingly, but death had no power over Him. Everything from the minutest details of His birth to His scornful death and miraculous resurrection had been written and foretold by the authors of the Old Testament centuries before He was born. **In Jesus** was the fulfillment of every prophecy concerning the Messiah, verifying that He was the **Savior of mankind.** John the Baptist proclaimed Him as the long-awaited Messiah, quoting directly from the Old Testament prophet Isaiah, who recognized Jesus as the long-awaited Messiah, "Behold, the Lamb of God who takes away the sins of the world" (John 1:29, John 1:36). That's why **Jesus is the foundation for my faith**; He is the **substance** of things hoped for, the **evidence** of things not seen. So what was **His message** and what was **His purpose?**

"And God said, '**Let us** make man in **our image**, after **our likeness**...
So God created mankind in **His** own image, in the image of God
**He** created them.'" (Genesis 1:26- 27)

## Chapter Three

# LET'S GO BACK TO THE BEGINNING

To better understand how we got to the point of mankind needing a savior, let's back up a little bit before we move on. Way back at the beginning of time and creation, a pivotal event took place that drastically changed the intended course of the human race, known as **the fall of man**. It came about when the harmonious relationship between God and man was broken because of **man's choice** to ignore the one and only restriction God gave him in spite of His stern warning. You see, God created man (and woman) in His own image in that they had **free will**; a conscience; personal feelings and emotions; the ability to make decisions; and the ability to interact with Him and relate to Him as their God and creator, with gratitude, respect, love, and trust. They also had the ability to interact with and relate to each other as well as future, fellow human beings with love, kindness, trust, mutual respect, and so on. "And **God** said, '**Let us** make man in **our image**, after **our likeness**. . . . So God created mankind **in His** own image, in the image of God **He** created them" (Genesis 1:26–27). Aside from the purpose of this verse in this context, of God creating man in His image, I love that verse because it displays the magnificence and complexity of God: His **oneness** as well as His **plurality**. It's beyond human comprehension, yet there it is.

Anyway, Ultimately **God's desire for mankind** was that as they learned from Him, trusted Him, and leaned on Him for guidance, they would experience a life full of love, goodness, peace, kindness, and joy. In harmony with their Creator, they would flourish and populate the earth, enjoying His fellowship as He would enjoy theirs, and mankind would be blessed with an abundance of everything good imaginable. Naturally, as you'd expect, they would acknowledge, trust, and honor Him as their God, the source of their very existence, and with that, everyone would live happily ever after. God's intention in creating mankind was to have a people He could call His own, to have fellowship with them, to have a relationship of mutual love between them. It was God's immeasurable love that inspired Him to create us. He gave us life as a gift: He lacked nothing but because of His great love, He wanted to share the experience; the kind of love that He had enjoyed from everlasting eternity- the perfect fellowship of love between The Father, The Son and the Holy Spirit. (Acts 17:24-26). However, there is no other way to achieve any kind of mutual, meaningful, or true relationship without **free will**. So God chose to give His creation free will, rather than to create mechanical or inanimate beings to be moved about the earth like trinkets on a board game. **Without free will**, the personal, intimate, and mutual relationship God desired **with** His creation, and **for** His creation, would be impossible. In fact, when you think about it, love is impossible without free will.

Anyway, their free will would soon be put to the test and reveal their character. God deeply loved His precious creation, and He abundantly blessed them, both Adam and Eve. He gave them reign over all of His creation, and as they strolled together with Him through their beautiful and perfect surroundings, God let them know that they could eat and enjoy everything in the flourishing garden, including the fruit from a very special tree in the center of the garden, which He referred to as the Tree of **Life**. God gave them only *one* exception, one thing that they **should avoid** at all costs, the cost of their very life, warning them that they should *not* eat of the fruit of one specific tree, which He referred to as the Tree of knowledge **of g**ood and evil. Without mincing words, God told them for their own good, as a loving Father warns their child of danger, that if they ate from that particular tree **"surely you shall die"** (Genesis 2:17). Sounds pretty straightforward. Easy enough, right? Eat it and **die**; don't eat it and **live** eternally and in perfect communion with God their Creator. Remember however, God gave them free will, giving them the **choice** to trust Him **or not**. Well, it wasn't long before God's beloved creation—first Eve, then Adam—made the consequential choice to disregard the **one and only** restriction He had given them for what sounded like a better offer. They made the choice to believe a smooth talking serpent instead of trusting God, their beloved Creator. That was **the original sin**, and from that moment on, everything was downhill. On that very day, they experienced **spiritual death**, being no longer in perfect communion with their Creator and their God, and ultimately **physical death** followed, because of that one decision, **just as God said it would**. God is a God of His word.

Throughout the ages, as one of the many excuses to reject the God of the Bible, mankind has stumbled over, argued, and questioned why a perfect God would create imperfect humans who could make a bad choice, as if they would have come up with a better idea. That argument always proves to be futile, and more than that, it clearly proves the pride and rebellion of mankind, thinking they know better than God. God knew exactly what He was doing. As I said before, **without free will**, the personal, intimate, and mutual relationship God desired **with** His creation and **for** His creation would be impossible. Quite simply, a mutual relationship of love cannot exist without free will. Adam and Eve's free will wasn't the problem; it was the fact that they used their free will to disobey God. Not only had God given them their very life and more than everything they needed, He had also given them fair warning of what would happen if they disobeyed Him. They should have trusted Him. Sadly they chose to listen to the smooth words of a serpent over the word of their beloved God, hence proving their character and sealing their fate.

**Death** was **never** intended for mankind, but rather it was the natural consequence of their choice. There they were, living in a perfect environment, living in perfect communion with God as He walked and talked with them in the Garden of Eden, having everything they needed, enjoying all that had been given to them, enjoying each other's company, naked and uninhibited; they were innocent and blameless before God without a hint of sorrow, guilt, or shame. Even with all that, they fell for **Satan's con job**. The serpent came to Eve in the garden first, shrewdly questioning her about the various trees in the garden. He smoothly and cleverly placed doubt in her, saying, "Did God *really* say that you should not eat of *every* tree of the garden?" (Genesis 3:1). Eve told him that God had allowed them to **eat freely of every tree,** with the exception of one: the tree of the knowledge of good and evil. Although as I was recently reading the account, I noticed that Eve added a curious addition to what God had actually said. This was God's warning to Adam: "Of every tree in the garden you may freely eat; but of the tree of the knowledge of good and evil **you shall not eat**, for in the day that you eat of it you shall surely die" (Genesis 2:17). However, in Eve's response to the serpent, she added a little something extra to the instruction that God had actually given to Adam. She told the serpent that God said, "You shall not eat it **nor shall you touch it**, lest you die" (Genesis 3:3). I don't know why she added the extra command ("nor shall you touch it") that God **had not** given; whether it came from Adam or what, I don't know. But I found it interesting, and it made me wonder if Eve hadn't already felt resentful about being restricted from the one tree before Satan even arrived in the garden. Anyway, Satan had her attention, and he made his move: he cunningly convinced her that God was trying to trick them and keep them from their full potential, insinuating that God had lied to them, and with a full display of confidence, Satan asserted, "Surely you would **not** die" (Genesis 3:4). He further spiced up his offer and sealed the deal by telling her that if they ate the fruit they would "gain all knowledge" and that they would "be like God" (Genesis 3:5). Eve was deceived, then she relayed the enticing information to Adam, who gladly chose to go along with his beloved wife and Satan's ruse.

The serpent was very crafty and seductive and, as it turned out, quite convincing, and apparently they were just **ambitious** enough to go for Satan's lies hook, line, and sinker—first Eve, then Adam.

So there they were, now faced with what they had done. They immediately tried to hide from God but to no avail. Naturally God knew exactly where they were and what they had done, and He confronted them. The fact that they tried to hide from God revealed their sense of shame, guilt, and sorrow, which they had never experienced before they disobeyed Him. Adding insult to injury, when God asked them about what they had done, Adam's first instinct was to pass the buck onto God and Eve saying, "The woman **You** gave me, **she** gave me fruit from the tree and I ate it" (Genesis 3:12). Naturally Eve followed suit by blaming the serpent for deceiving her: "**The serpent deceived me** and I ate." (Genesis 3:13). Eve basically said to God, "The devil made me do it." Although this was really no surprise to God, I always picture Him standing there shaking His head in disappointment.

**The bottom line is this**: by their own free will, Adam and Eve **chose** to believe what the serpent told them instead of believing what God had told them, and they knew **the truth**—that they had **no one to blame but themselves**. They felt the heavy weight of what they had done pressing down on them in that moment. From that day forward, as descendants of Adam and Eve, **all** men (and women) have been born into sin. That's just who they were, and their bloodline has been passed down to us. In other words, it is as though **sin** is now part of **our** spiritual **DNA**. As unflattering as it may sound, we're *all* sinners by nature.

So as we can see, Adam and Eve lived in a perfect environment, they had absolutely everything they needed, they were in perfect communion with God, they lacked nothing. Still, with their own free will, when given the choice, they wanted more. The truth is this: we can't blame the world, the environment; we can't even blame the devil—or anything else. It was the natural character of Adam and Eve, and the same for us, because of our ancestry—but thanks be to God for loving us and for saving us from our own eternal destruction, for giving each of us a second chance to get it right. You could say Adam and Eve failed the test; they just didn't make the mark. God could have just moved on; He could have "scrapped the project," so to speak, right then and there in the garden. *But He didn't.* He had a strong compassion and a deep love for His creation, and because of His compassion and His love, there was hope for mankind. The reality is that God being God, He knew exactly what would happen, He knew exactly what they would do. When you consider that, He could also have "skipped the project" altogether. ***But He didn't.*** We can spend our time saying "That's not fair, I didn't ask to be born," but it won't change a thing. Because here we are. We've been given our life, and we're told that it's a gift from God. It's our choice how we want to use the gift. Apparently some things just have to play out to get to the ultimate result. Without claiming to have all the answers, based on the information we've been given, apparently God felt that having a relationship with mankind was a worthwhile cause in spite of their inevitable faulty character. And He provided a way of redemption for us all that satisfied His own requirement of justice.

Although Adam and Eve were banished from the garden, they would reap the consequences of their decision, and along the way they would learn some serious lessons in humility, **God stayed with them** through it all. They realized that they had screwed up and they accepted that they, as well as their future generations, would now have to labor and suffer through life as the natural consequence of their decision to ignore God's instruction. Adam and Eve's disobedience had brought sin into the world and severely damaged their relationship with their Creator, but the damage would not be permanent. God let them know that He still loved them, and although it was going to be a long, rough road for a while, He would be with them every step of the way if they would continue to trust Him. God had compassion on them, He felt sorry for them, as He understood their frailties. He also had a plan all along, to help them out of the mess they'd gotten themselves into because of their sinful nature—a plan that would ultimately **bridge the gap between God and man.** God is omniscient, so He knew exactly what would happen. But as I said, because of His deep love for His creation, God felt that having a relationship with mankind was a worthwhile cause.

Anyway, as time passed—through His chosen people and prophets—God filled His beloved mankind in on His plan. God promised them a King who would be their Savior; He would be born into the world and He would lift the heavy weight of their sin from them forever and **restore their relationship with Him.** God Himself would provide the necessary and only acceptable sacrifice that would provide forgiveness "once and for all" for the sins of all mankind (Romans 6:10, Hebrews 10:12). Although they didn't know it at the time, **Jesus** was that long-awaited promise—God Himself, clothed in humanity.

So as the world continued to populate, there were the people of God, *humble* men and women who remembered and learned the lesson from the garden as they were passed down from their forefathers. They understood that their DNA was tainted with sin while they fumbled through life trying their best to acknowledge God, to follow His ways, and to trust Him through many years of adversity. God continued along patiently with His beloved people, helping them to understand the severity of sin and the ruin and destruction it brings, teaching them about His preordained laws, letting them know the requirement of blood, explaining to them its significance: "The life of the flesh is in the blood" (Leviticus 17:11). God began to teach them through a system of sacrifice using the blood of goats and lambs and various animals as they learned the important lesson that "without the shedding of blood, there is no forgiveness of sins" (Leviticus 17:11, Hebrews 9:22). Through all of this, they began to understand the *holiness and the loving kindness* of their God. Meanwhile they held tightly to **God's promise of a Savior**, the Lamb of God who would be the final sacrifice for the sins of mankind. The symbolic blood of animals one day would no longer be needed when God Himself would take care of the sins of mankind. And as you might expect, there were still those who persisted in their rebellion against God; they continued down the path of Satan's deceptions. Instead of learning the lessons of their forefathers, they were arrogant, *full of pride*, and refused to acknowledge or obey God, living under their own authority, answering to no one, running amuck entertaining demons, entrenched in sorcery, and engaging in every kind of immoral behavior imaginable. And they were thoroughly enjoying their depravation, relentless in their empty quest to be like God, and in some cases to replace Him, worshipping at the feet of images and idols. Which reminds us as we look at the world today that the more things change, the more they stay the same.

Moving on—Centuries passed, kingdoms and civilizations rose and fell, and in the fullness of time, **Jesus**, the long-awaited Savior of the world, was finally born in a lowly manger among the sheep and cattle. Jesus didn't fit the expectations of the religious leaders of the day, although during that time, there were many Jews who knew the scriptures of the Old Testament Prophets who wrote of a "suffering servant," and they recognized Jesus as the Son of God, and accepted Him as their Messiah, *and many more have since, and will continue to come to Him* in the future. The religious leaders, and the nation of Israel as a whole would not accept Him, they rejected Him when He was in their very midst; and His salvation was further extended to the gentiles of that day and forward. He'll get back to His own people, the Nation of Israel in due time.

Jesus lived His life on earth *according to the will of His Father* in heaven. Jesus, the Lamb of God being the final sacrifice for the sins of mankind, fulfilled his life-saving mission with His own blood through His death on the cross. He was resurrected from death to life, validating His divine nature as the only begotten Son of God. He then ascended to His rightful place in heaven **with the promise to return.** Jesus came into the world the **first time** as a gentle, loving **Savior**, offering salvation and eternal life to all who would accept it. However, according to the scriptures, when He returns the **second time**, He will arrive on the scene as a mighty warrior and **Judge**. He will be returning to judge those who have willfully rejected Him as their Savior, as it's vividly and graphically described in the Book of Revelation. His judgment will be severe, righteous, thorough, and perfect. Once His judgment is complete, Jesus will then establish His Kingdom **on earth as it is in heaven.** During that time, the earth will be restored to perfection, brought back to the lush likes of the Garden of Eden, and Jesus Himself will reign as King for a millennium, in fulfillment of His promise to the Nation of Israel. Ruling with Him will be all those from **every** generation **past** and **present** who desired a relationship with God, by trusting in His Son, Jesus, for their salvation. After the thousand-year reign of Christ on earth, every believer will enter their eternal destination, the magnificent place we know as heaven, and there, they will forever be with their God and their Savior for eternity. Those who chose not to believe will be sent to their eternal destiny as well. The fact is this: we are eternal beings and we are all destined for eternity, and we each will choose our own destiny. For practical purposes, I've given you the *very condensed* version of the history of mankind and God's plan for the future. God is not slow to fulfill His promises, but rather He is patient and merciful, giving **every opportunity** until His appointed time to return. Keep this in mind: God is not bound in time as we are; God is eternal. The apostle Peter reminds us, "With the Lord a day is like a thousand years, and a thousand years like a day" (2 Peter 3:8).

To sum it up: Through the first man, **Adam**, sin was brought into the world, and indiscriminately passed on to **all** mankind. In other words, when it comes to sin, like it or lump it, we've got it, to one degree or another. It's in our bloodline. Through Adam, **sin** entered the world. Through **Jesus**, the Son of God, who came to the world in the form of a man, salvation was brought into the world, and through Him redemption is offered to all mankind. "For as by one man's disobedience many were made sinners, so also by one Man's obedience many will be made righteous. Moreover the law entered that the offense might abound. But where sin abounded, grace abounded much more. So that as sin reigned in death, even so grace might reign through Jesus Christ our Lord" (Romans 5:19).

However, **unlike sin,** redemption is **not** indiscriminately passed on to all mankind. God has given the human race a second chance on a "case-by-case basis" so to speak. Everyone must make a personal choice. There's that darn **free will** again. Through this divine plan, God's desire will become a reality: to have a people of His own that He can enjoy a mutually loving relationship with, in a perfect place without the stain and destruction of sin; it will be a perfect paradise. Through God's divine plan, there will be no doubt as to those who really want to be with Him for eternity and those who prefer to go their own way. Redemption and the permanent forgiveness of our sins with the promise of eternal life requires an individual choice, a personal decision to accept the need and desire for the gift offered or to reject it and hope for the best. Because God is omniscient, He already knows those who will accept His offer as well as those who will reject it, but as for us, God's plan will play out for everyone to see as the spiritual warfare between God and Satan continues. "For God so loved the world that He gave His only begotten Son, that **whoever believes in Him** should not perish but have everlasting life" (John 3:16). "If you shall **confess with your mouth** the Lord Jesus, and shall **believe in your heart** that God has raised Him from the dead, you shall be saved" (Romans 10:9).

"For our struggle is not against flesh and blood, but against the rulers, against the authorities, against **the powers of this dark world,** and against **the spiritual forces of evil** in the heavenly realms. (Ephesians 6:12)

## Chapter Four

## MEANWHILE, BACK ON THE EARTH . . .

Meanwhile, until God's plan comes to full fruition, until **Jesus returns** for His people, Satan—described as the evil one, the great deceiver, the father of lies—is still **alive and well** and continues his spiritual warfare in our world today. Make no mistake: there is an invisible battle for your soul taking place as we speak, and although invisible, it's very real and more dangerous than any physical battle you'll ever find yourself in. When I was a little girl, I remember a song I learned in the first or second grade called "Who Has Seen the Wind?" The first line went like this: "Who has seen the wind, neither you nor I, but when the trees bow down their heads, the wind is passing by." Like the wind, the same is with "the invisible battle" that is taking place in our midst: there is so much going on in the spiritual realm that we can't see with our eyes, but the results are very tangible. Although the demonic spiritual forces would be better compared to a tornado that rips trees out of the ground by their roots rather than bowing their heads. Regarding this battle, the apostle Paul tells us exactly what we're dealing with: "For our struggle is not against flesh and blood, but against the rulers, against the authorities, against **the powers of this dark world**, and against **the spiritual forces of evil** in the heavenly realms" (Ephesians 6:12). The apostle Peter explains why we need to be diligent and aware: "So be alert and **sober of mind.** Your enemy the devil prowls around like a roaring lion seeking someone to devour" (1 Peter 5:8). Paul also reminds us, "Satan himself **masquerades** as an angel of light" (2 Corinthians 11:14). There's an equally interesting backstory about Satan and how he ended up in the garden and about the rest of the fallen angels working with him, but I won't get into that at this time. However, **no one can deny the existence of *evil* in the world today.** Satan and his army of demons are at the bottom of it all and have been up to no good since they got themselves thrown out of heaven. They've successfully confused and deceived the world even to the point that evil looks good and good looks evil. They have no plans of letting up, and you can be sure they'll continue to stir up trouble through the end of the age. Their powers are only second to God's and **can't be** underestimated. Satan knows all too well the character of mankind; he knows just how weak they are and how easily they will fall for anything with the slightest persuasion. Satan is still using the same tactics and lures that he used in the garden to entice the human race. He is still using <u>temptation.</u> Remember his *tempting* words to Eve? "You will gain all knowledge" and "You can be like God." Aside from the fact that mankind as a whole, continues to call their own shots, with the attitude toward God that says "You're not the boss of me," we can see through the rapid advancement of technology, this is still the ultimate quest of mankind, **to be like God:** with the artificially intelligent beings that are so realistic that you can hardly tell they're robots; as well as the tampering with DNA in a pursuit to create made-to-order designer babies. Even well-known superstars are having their pets cloned. I could go on, but I think you get the picture. There's no doubt in my mind that all of this "artificial intelligence" comes straight from the pit of hell. There's no denying that mankind wants to be God. Mankind as a whole continues in their quest, refusing to accept His authority and refusing to acknowledge that *without* Him, for as long as they continue to rebel *against* Him, they can **never be like** Him. Satan is still using <u>doubt</u>. Remember what he said to Eve through the serpent: "Did God *really* say that . . . ?" He's and his army of demons are still placing doubt in the minds of the world today. And they will continue to use various forms of <u>deception</u>. He lied with confidence, saying to Eve, "Surely you will not die." Liar, liar, pants on fire! Jesus called Satan the father of lies when He was speaking to the religious leaders: "You are of your father, the devil, and the lust of your father will you do. He was a murderer from the beginning, not holding to the truth, for **there is no truth in him.** When he lies he speaks his native language, for he is a liar and the **father of lies**" (John 8:44–45). And Satan's deception continues.

Satan is the very **essence of evil**, and we're warned that he will manifest himself as a roaring lion or even an angel of light and anything in between. The unseen spiritual forces of evil are in full force today just as when they began in the garden. Satan and his full army of demons continue their work in the world today—using every *diversion*, from technology to travel; every *distraction*, from astrology to aliens; and every *deception* imaginable, from psychics and sorcery to evolution and reincarnation. They'll use various forms of entertainment and even the mundane activities of life, doing whatever it takes to steer people away from **the truth of God**. But regardless, the truth will remain the same and will prevail in the end. Satan is also referred to as the god of this world: "**the god of this world** who has blinded the minds of unbelievers, so that they cannot see the light of the gospel that reveals the glory of **Christ who is the very image of God**" (2 Corinthians 4:4). Satan's only mission is to steal, kill, and destroy while he still has the time. And he is well aware that his time is running short. Although remember, we can't blame Satan any more than Adam and Eve could. We have the same *free will*, the choice to believe God or to believe Satan, as the saga and the spiritual struggle between God and Satan continues.

"Come now, and let us reason together, saith the Lord: though your sins be as scarlet, they shall be as white as snow; though they be like crimson, they shall be as wool. (Isaiah 1:18)

## Chapter Five

## THE MIRACLE SPOT REMOVER

So that's where it all began, and here we are now. We've all said or heard this commonly used phrase at one time or another: "Nobody's perfect." Our innermost being knows that simple truth—nobody's perfect. The commonly used phrases "Nobody's perfect" and "We're only human" are very telling; they're excuses for whatever it is that we fall short of. Those are mankind's go-to lines when we fall short and don't live up to our own or others' expectations. What's **clear** in those proclamations is that the human race understands at its very core that there is a **higher standard** (which is perfect) that we have **yet** to attain. Do you ever wonder where that higher standard came from? That universal and core understanding is the very thing that God has put in each of our hearts and has placed into our consciences for the single purpose of drawing us, mankind, to Himself.

Confirming what we already know, we're told in the Old Testament that "All of us like sheep have gone astray, each has turned to his own way" (Isaiah 53:6). Again, in the New Testament we're told that "all have sinned and fallen short of the Glory of God" (Romans. 3:23). It doesn't say "some of us" or "most of us" but **all of us** have gone astray, **all** have sinned and fallen short. The apostle John tells us this: "If we say we have no sin, we deceive ourselves, and the **truth** is not in us" (John 1:8). Now, here's the problem with sin and the fact that nobody's perfect: We're told that there is a price, a serious penalty to pay for our imperfections. According to the law of God, "The wages of sin is death" (Romans 6:23). From a human perspective, that may sound **harsh** because sin is second nature to us. However, from a heavenly perspective, from the perspective of a Perfect and Holy God, things look very different. Have you ever had a tiny spot of soy sauce on a pure, white sweater? You may try and try to get the spot out, but it just can't be removed. Although you love the sweater, eventually you either stop wearing it altogether or you just throw it out; all because of a tiny little spot that is barely visible to anyone else, but it is very visible to you. You just **can't** overlook it. It's kind of like that. Think of that tiny little spot on your favorite pure, white sweater that you couldn't overlook. Now think about how much more disturbing the sin of the world would be to a **H**oly, **R**ighteous, and **P**erfect **G**od. Because of God's own nature of **H**oliness, He has a "zero tolerance policy" on sin, and **He** can't overlook it. But God, in His mercy, made a way to remove the spot, so to speak, making it white as snow, as if it were never there. "Come now, and let us reason together, saith the Lord: though your sins be as scarlet, they shall be as white as snow; though they be like crimson, they shall be as wool" (Isaiah 1:18). **Jesus** is the miracle spot remover. "The wages of sin is death, [but thankfully] the gift of God is Eternal Life **in Jesus Christ**" (Romans 6:23). Revealing that God is not only **righteous** and **just** but His **compassion** and **mercy** are immeasurable. What does this mean, and how does it apply to you and me?

Very simply put, regarding God's requirement of perfection is this example: In the same way a surgeon is not permitted to enter a germ-free surgical room without thoroughly scrubbing himself with disinfectant soap and clothing himself in a sterile gown, according to God, we can't enter heaven—a sin-free, perfect, and holy environment—unless we are thoroughly cleansed and clothed in perfection. But since "nobody's perfect," how can we enter? God Himself satisfied His required *debt* for our sin, which is *death*. Thereby confirming His standard of **h**oliness and **r**ighteousness and His **p**erfect **j**ustice. The debt has been satisfied. Justice has been served. His sacrificial act also confirmed His love and His mercy for us, because He took our place, **shedding His own blood** so that we may have forgiveness for our sins and Eternal Life. Although "The wages of sin is death . . . the gift of God is Eternal Life in Jesus Christ." That's what this means, that's the deal; you don't have to work for it, earn it, or hope that you're good enough. God has already done it all. **Paid in full at the cross!**

God's mercy and grace are so amazing; I can explain it like this: Picture a man who is **guilty,** he's sitting on **death row** awaiting his execution when the guard flings open his cell door and says, "Hey, buddy, you're off the hook. Someone else has taken your place. A kind-hearted, compassionate man stepped in on your behalf. *He has just been executed in your place*, so your slate is clean and you're free to go." The man steps out of his cell and into the free world, amazed, eternally grateful, a new man without a single charge against him. **He** is no longer counted as guilty because the debt **he** owed has been satisfied by someone else, an **innocent man**, who took his place. The guard even gives him a special parting gift as he walks out of the prison doors, sending him into the world with his own helper and advocate to assist him on a daily basis, like a moral compass to help keep him out of future trouble. Wow, imagine that!

"And when I saw Him, I fell at His feet as dead. But He laid His right
hand on me, saying to me, 'Do not be afraid: I am the first and the last.
I am He who lives and was dead, and behold, I am alive forevermore.
Amen. (Revelation 1:17-18)

# Chapter Six

## "THERE AIN'T NO GRAVE . . ."

Through Adam and Eve's disobedience, the separation between man and God, known as **spiritual death**, occurred, as did **physical death**, and both were inherited and passed on to us. But God's divine plan would offer mankind a **spiritual rebirth** through faith in Him as well as a **physical rebirth** in the promise of our own resurrection into eternal life. All of this was made possible because of **Jesus**. The fact that Jesus lifted Himself from the grave gives me full confidence that He will do the same for me and all those who believe—because He said He would.

You probably noticed a lot of talk about the subject of death. I realize that death is not a very popular subject, and you may have been wondering, "Where is she going with all this talk about death?" My intention was not to be negative or morbid but to bring hope to people at a common place, a place that everyone can relate to. I don't know anyone who hasn't been touched by death in one way or another, whether it be the loss of a family member, a close friend, a neighbor, or even a beloved actor, athlete, musician or well-known celebrity. At my age it seems that barely a month goes by that I don't hear about someone else from my own family or circle of life who has died. In spite of that reality, there is hope and a light at the end of the tunnel. For the human race, death is a problem we can all relate to, and Jesus is the solution to that problem because **Jesus defeated death**. He has offered the same to us, giving **us** hope for the future and victory over the grave. When I use the word *hope*, I'm not using it lightly, as in "I sure hope this or that happens." When I say *hope*, I mean that we look forward with great anticipation to specific promises that have their roots in miraculous events of the Living Son of God Almighty! The light at the end of the tunnel is Jesus, the *light* of the world. My hope is firmly placed on the Rock of ages, *Jesus*, the one who walked out of his own grave! As one songwriter put it, "There aint no grave gonna hold my body down! If Jesus walked out of the grave, I'm walkin' too!" That's the promise and the victory we have in Jesus.

25

I heard that a popular Atheist website wrote a comment regarding Christians using Scripture as an authority, saying: "All they've got is just a bunch of Bible verses." Those verses wouldn't have any value or authority without the proper endorsement. The account of the origin of man as recorded in the Bible has been passed off or dismissed by some as mere fable. **Had it not been for Jesus**, I may be tempted to do the same. However, **Jesus confirmed** the authority, reliability, and veracity of the scriptures as chronicled by the Old Testament prophets, proclaiming them *an authority* and referring to them as **truth**. And Jesus validated Himself as the Son of the living God and **the Savior of mankind** throughout His life and ministry of miracles; recorded and preserved for us, and ending with the grand finale of His Own miraculous resurrection **from death to life**. No other person or spiritual leader has done that. **Only God can do that.**

God saw our condition, and because of His compassion and love for us, He made a way. Because of His mercy on us, He offered a provision for us to enter heaven in spite of our imperfections. God reconciled Himself to us according to His own laws, and He personally took care of His required debt for our imperfections—a spiritual cleansing, so to speak. God stepped in on our behalf, wiping our slate clean, making us perfect and suitable for heaven. He did this because He loves us and He desires a relationship with us. All I had to do was accept the gift and let God handle the rest.

Within the mysteries and complexities of the scriptures echo these simple messages from God to us: "God so loved the world that He gave His only begotten Son, that whosoever believes in Him shall not perish, but have everlasting life" (John 3:16). "For by grace you are **saved** through faith; **not** of yourselves: it is the **gift** of God" (Ephesians 2:8–9). Jesus said, "I am the resurrection and the life. He who believes in Me, **though he may die, he shall live.** And whoever lives and believes in Me shall never die." (John 11:25-26). He said, "I am the **way**, the **truth** and the **life. No man** comes to the Father **but by me**" (John 14:6). He said, "I am the light of the world. Whosoever follows me will never walk in darkness, but will have the light of life" (John 8:12). He said, "In My Father's house are many mansions . . . I go to prepare a place for you, that where I am you may be also . . ." (John 14:2). "Believe on the Lord Jesus Christ and you shall be saved" (Acts 16:31). These are some pretty bold statements. So why do I believe this? I believe because those words come on **good authority**.

"He will wipe away every tear from their eyes, and there will be no more death or mourning or crying or pain, for the former things have passed away. And the One seated on the throne said 'Behold I make all things new." (Revelation 21:4-5)

# Chapter Seven

## AND THEY LIVED HAPPILY EVER AFTER!

Talk is cheap. Many spiritual leaders and prophets have made outrageous claims throughout the centuries, but **Jesus, unlike anyone else in the history of mankind**, put His money where His mouth is, so to speak. He offered rock-solid, undeniable proof, recorded in our history. That's why I speak of Jesus with confidence—it's because of Who He is and what He's done. He substantiated His claims **as only God could do**: *by conquering death itself*!

No religious leader, no philosopher or prophet, no other spiritual leader, no shaman, guru, pope, or high priest, carries those kinds of credentials. Like the sign along the road said, "Why go anywhere else?" Speaking of Jesus, the apostle John said, "In the beginning was **the Word** and the Word was **with God** and the Word **was God** . . . and the Word **became flesh** and dwelt among us" (John 1:1, John 1:14). The very thought of that one truth is overwhelming—to think of the Eternal Son of God, the living Word of God who **was** from the beginning, Who **is** God Himself–to think of Him leaving His place of glory, becoming flesh, and dwelling among His own creation in order to save them. Wow! It's truly mind-boggling and incredible, but this is what He did. The apostle Paul, who came face-to-face with the resurrected and glorified Jesus on the road to Damascus while he was on the way to capture, torture, and kill Christians, tells us this about Jesus: "**In Him** dwells all the fullness of God in bodily form" (Colossians 2:9). Jesus said, "If you have seen Me you have seen the Father" and "I and My Father are one" (John 14:7–14). Jesus proclaims, "I am the Alpha and the Omega, the Beginning and the End, who is and who was and who is to come, the Almighty" (Revelation 1:8). The apostle John's account: "And when I saw Him, I fell at His feet as dead. But He laid His right hand on me, saying to me, 'Do not be afraid: I am the first and the last. I am He who lives and was dead, and behold, I am alive forevermore. Amen. And I have the keys of Hades and death'" (Revelation 1:17–18).

The thought of all these things is unfathomable and a lot to wrap my head around. And I don't dare claim to understand all the complexities of God, the incredible oneness of the Father, the Son, and the Holy Spirit. He is God and it is the foolishness and pride of mankind to attempt to explain Him or fit Him into our finite understanding. It's impossible for me to answer every question or explain all the intricacies of His divine plan, for they're far beyond my understanding. However, the core of His message was clear and direct: "God so loved the world that He gave His only begotten Son. Whosoever believeth in Him shall not perish but have everlasting life" (John 3:16). *That* I understand. He offered His own resurrection from death to life as proof. Not only do we have the promise of eternal life giving us hope beyond the grave, but we have the promise of a life right here and now, filled with *joy*, peace, love, and strength even in the midst of deep sorrow because we know how the story ends. I don't know about you, but I love a happy ending.

This brings to mind a very dear friend of mine who loves to read. She's always in the middle of one book or another. She shared something with me that I thought was so funny at the time, but I get it. She said that sometimes when she's getting into a good book that takes a turn that she didn't see coming or the characters that she's become attached to don't seem to be going in the direction she's hoping for, she can't read on! She'll stop and go to the end of the book to see how it works out before she decides if she wants to finish the story. She just loves a happy ending too. Thanks be to God; we can all find comfort when things seem uncertain and trouble surrounds us because we can **know** the ending of our story. "He will wipe away every tear from their eyes, and there will be no more death or mourning or crying or pain, for the former things have passed away. And the one who sits on the throne said 'Behold, I make all things new.'" (Revelation 21:4-6) Simply put, the ending goes something like this: "All their sorrows were over; and they all lived happily ever after." Now that's something to look forward to! The offer is for everyone, the gift is free, but the choice is ours to take it or leave it.

"This is the judgement, that the light has come into the world, and people loved the darkness rather than the light because their deeds were evil...they do not come to the light lest their deeds be exposed."
(John 3:19)

## *Chapter Eight*

## WHAT'S *YOUR* PROBLEM–WITH JESUS?

I find this interesting, but it's been my observation that people are very comfortable discussing or embracing various philosophies and religions—anything from witchcraft to New Age spiritualism—but they become noticeably uncomfortable at the mention of **Jesus**. You can almost see them looking around for the nearest exit, or they can't change the subject fast enough. For others the subject causes them to be overtly cutting, sarcastic, condescending, and even hateful at times. The apostle Peter tells us that many will find Jesus to be "a stone of stumbling and a rock of offense" (1 Peter2:8). What is it about the subject of **Jesus** that causes such discomfort? A couple things come to mind: Jesus said "I am **the light** of the world, whoever follows me will never walk in darkness but he shall have the light of life" (John 8:12). Now, Satan on the other hand is called, among other things, the prince of **darkness**. Remember his mission is to **keep** people **in darkness**. "The god of this world has **blinded** the minds of unbelievers, **to keep them from seeing** the light of the gospel of the glory of Jesus Christ, who is the very image of God" (2 Corinthians 4:4). So here we can see the two extreme opposites, *in their characteristics*: One is **light** and the other **darkness**–One entirely **good** and the other entirely **evil**.

When we think of light and its attributes, we think of it shining; illuminating; bringing awareness, clarity and revelation; exposing things you may not have seen without the light. Have you ever seen a ray or beam of light coming through your window, and within that ray of light, you see there are millions of tiny little dust particles? Then you look around at the furniture in the room and you realize that it's covered in dust too! Of course, you know that the beam of light didn't bring the dust in, but rather that the light **exposed it** to you. At that point you can get out your dust rag or you can close the blinds. The apostle John, speaking again of light and darkness, brought up an interesting explanation as to why people so strongly reject Jesus. "This is **the judgement**, that the light has come into the world, and people loved the darkness rather than the light because their deeds were evil... they do not come to the light lest their deeds be exposed" (John 3:19). Most who hear that will quickly jump to their own defense: " Surely he's not talking about me! I'm a 'good person." Most of us, even **if** we consider our own sin, don't think of it as "evil." But God, being perfect and holy—not to mention all-knowing—has a very different idea about what evil is. According to God, *anything* outside of His perfect will is considered evil to one degree or another. Remember your favorite pure, white sweater that *you* threw out – **not** because of a *big splat*, but because of a *tiny, little* spot?

I mentioned those two opposing beings of light and darkness and good and evil. But understand, that while they may be two opposing beings, they're *not* equal in power—*not even close*. So many times we see action movies or dramas depicting the battle between the two forces as if they are two equally powerful forces battling it out. But let me assure you, **Satan is no match for God**, and he literally trembles at the name of **Jesus**. God is the Creator, Satan was created, and that still ticks him off. God is all-powerful, His power has *no limitations*, while Satan's power is *very* limited by comparison. This world *for now*, is under the dominion of Satan, however, his time is running out. Ultimately, evil cannot overcome goodness any more than darkness can overcome light. God's goodness, light, and power will prevail. Through the scriptures we have the advantage of knowing who wins in the end (spoiler alert: it's *not* Satan. He's going down!). The bottom line is that some people will continue to come up with various reasons to reject Jesus and some will hear His voice and respond to His call. The struggle for each soul continues and is all rooted in the spiritual warfare that began in the garden; the age-old battle between **truth** and **deception** that we are in the midst of even now. And the outcome of each man's eternal destiny will be determined by *the heart* of each individual and whether they will reject the truth or embrace it.

Many who reject Jesus are quick to point out **atrocities** done in the name of Christianity or **hypocrisy** among Christian leaders, church members, even family members or followers as a reason or an excuse to steer clear and reject anything to do with "organized religion." However, Christianity is **not** a religion; it is a relationship with God through His only begotten Son, Jesus; who has claimed to be "**the** Way, **the** Truth, and **the** Life." Jesus did *not* say, "Follow me. I am one of **many** ways." On the contrary, Jesus said, "I am *the* way." Jesus claimed that He is the *only* way. To make sure that everyone was clear, He further added, "**No man** comes to the Father **but by me**." Religion is all about what *you do*—Christianity is all about what **Jesus** has already *done*.

Christianity stands **solely on the person of Jesus**, and Jesus was not a hypocrite. He lived His entire life consistently with what He taught. He willingly came from His rightful place in heaven, to this earth on a mission to save mankind, and He completed it. As He hung on the cross, in His last breath, Jesus spoke these words: "It is finished" (John 19:30). In other words, mission accomplished! Jesus, who had **no** sin in Him, became sin, that we might be made the righteousness of God in Him (2 Corinthians 5:21). He did this to save us from eternal torment and separation from God. Jesus is the Eternal God, the Creator of all things, Who **was,** and **is,** and forever **will be.** He is the same God who spoke to the Prophet, Moses in the Old Testament referring to Himself as I AM. "Then Moses asked God, 'Suppose I go to the Israelites and say to them, The God of your fathers has sent me to you, and they ask me, What is His name? What should I tell them?' God said to Moses, 'I AM WHO I AM. This is what you are to say to the Israelites: I AM has sent you.'" (Exodus 3:13-14). While being questioned and taunted by the Jewish Leaders, Jesus declared this: "Truly, truly I tell you, before Abraham was born, I AM." (John 8:58). At that point they picked up stones to kill Him; knowing the Old Testament scriptures, they knew exactly what He was saying, He was claiming to be the Eternal God which was considered blasphemy. Jesus *willingly* stepped out of a boundless state of *eternity* into the boundaries of *time and space,* came to earth and humbly clothed Himself in humanity for a short time in history for a *single purpose*: to save mankind. His followers are mere humans born into sin; **they** are **not** perfect. I can only hope and pray that the inadequacies or failings of Christians, including myself, would not be used as a reason or excuse to keep anyone from accepting Christ and being saved into eternal life. Christianity hinges on **Jesus** and **His** accomplishments: His birth, His life, His earthly ministry, His death, and most importantly His resurrection and His ascension into heaven—all for our benefit and all confirming His divine nature. Christianity *does not* stand or rest on the behavior of its followers. In a world where hypocrisy is everywhere and can be found throughout many organizations, it seems unfair and even hypocritical, in and of itself to invalidate the Christian faith, pointing out hypocrisy among followers as a means of rejecting it. No amount of hypocrisy among His followers will change a single fact about **Jesus** or the claims He made.

"This is My commandment, that you love one another
as I have loved you. Greater love has no one than this,
than to lay down his life for his friends." (John 15:12-13)

## *Chapter Nine*

## NO GREATER LOVE

There are also people who will tell you that they don't like Christian churches or groups, complaining that they come across as **self-righteous, judgmental, and legalistic** (no smoking, no drinking, no rock 'n' roll, no dancing, no cussing, and the list of dos and don'ts goes on). Although perhaps well intended, and in some cases good advice, unfortunately God's love can be lost in legalism; His message of **grace** gets all muddled in a cloud of condemnation and rules. No doubt some churches are full of high-minded busybodies who spend their time in gossip and petty judgment. There's no room for such behavior in any Christian church. Aside from the fact that it may cause division among church members, it may become a stumbling block for newcomers who have come to church to find the truth and the love of God.

However, with all that said, I would think that someone attending a Christian church would expect to hear about the grace of God, which would mean absolutely nothing if there wasn't a **need** for God's grace. And there would be no need for God's grace if there was no sin. So you see, grace and sin go hand in hand, God's **grace** being the free gift of God and the only provision for the forgiveness of **sin**. So it shouldn't surprise anyone to hear about **sin** right along with love and grace when they attend a true Christian Church. That is the entire point of the gospel? Just remember this: God is our only Judge and He is also our only Savior. We're told that "God demonstrates His own love toward us, in that while we were yet sinners, Christ died for us" (Romans 5:8). In other words, Jesus was entirely aware of our imperfections, our most well-hidden sins, when He sacrificed His own life to save us. "There is no greater love than this" (John 15:13–14).

Christians are told to speak the *truth* in love. But many completely *neglect* the truth in the *name* of "love." As much as we are to love one another, we realize that God is **not** an anything-goes God, and He does have a purpose and a standard for our lives. That standard is found within His word and what we (should) strive toward as Christians. Naturally a perfect and holy God has a standard as to how we should conduct ourselves: how we should speak to one another, about the language we use, about what we fill our time and even our minds with, about various subjects of morality, and so on. But just to be crystal-clear, we understand completely that we are saved **solely** by our faith in Jesus. Remember He fully understands our inability to perfectly uphold His standards. We know that we are *not* saved by our good behavior or we'd all be in trouble. "For whoever keeps the whole law and yet stumbles at one point is guilty of all" (James 2:10). In other words, it's not that we are striving toward a standard or following a bunch of rules **as a means** of working **for** our salvation; rather with the help of the Holy Spirit of God, we're working at doing the will of God as **a result of** our salvation. It's kind of like this: "You can bark all day long and that won't make you a dog. However, if you're a dog, you will bark because that's what dogs do."

There are many go-to verses in the Bible that people will often rattle off when it's convenient that tell us not to judge one another: "Judge not lest you be judged" (Matthew 7:1, Luke 6:37). "Why do you look at the speck of sawdust in your brother's eye and pay no attention to the plank in your own eye?" (Matthew 7:3). "He who is without sin, let him cast the first stone" (John 8:7). However, if you're truly God's child, you'll want to know what He has to say, you'll appreciate godly instruction from other believers when it is given in love.

Christians who have tuned in to the word of God understand that **Sin is a reality**, and without the amazing grace of God, which is only found in Jesus**, no one** is exempt from its penalty. After all, Jesus willingly came to earth to give His life as a sacrifice for the sins of mankind—yours, mine, and everyone's—so it seems absolutely appropriate, if not necessary, to **call a sin a sin**, and you should expect to hear about it if you attend a true Christian church. For once the problem (of sin) is recognized, it's then we are turned to God's grace and mercy for the solution to the problem and allow His grace to transform us. Although Christians will make mistakes, as they grow in the knowledge of God's grace, they will not be comfortable living in a continuous state of rebellion. They will be in a constant conflict and struggle with the Spirit of God who inhabits them, He will be continually convicting their hearts, drawing them back to the narrow road.

It's the job of the Holy Spirit of God to convict, the heart of each individual, and our job as believers **to love one another**, to keep the planks out of our own eyes before picking at the speck in anyone else's. We should pray for fellow believers and unbelievers alike, for all those who are struggling with sin in various areas and times of their lives. God knows that we will never be perfect while we are in this world, but from the moment we place our faith in **Jesus**, when we humbly come to Him **in faith** exactly as we are, with all our imperfections, we are **immediately counted as perfect** in God's eyes forevermore. That's the amazing *grace* of God! The Spirit of God *seals our salvation* the moment we truly believe in our hearts. (Ephesians 1:13, Ephesians 4:30). He is our helper, our advocate and resides within each believer; He begins His miraculous and personal transformation as we yield to His will and lean on Him for guidance. By that same token, we don't want to grieve the Spirit of God, and I speak from my own experience; we find, we grieve ourselves when we do. We are sure to stunt our own spiritual growth, take some dangerous turns, and reap the consequences when we don't follow His lead. Thinking back on the times in my life when I would have appreciated some gentle, godly guidance. Thankfully God is so patient with us. When a person is born into the family of God through faith in Jesus, **we** should be patient too. Realizing that much like a newborn baby will learn, grow, and develop physically, each new-born Christian will be growing and developing at his or her own spiritual rate too, and we should understand that there will be setbacks and mistakes along the way as well. They're still learning. We all are. Don't sit back and judge them; talk *to* them, not *about* them; confront them gently if you see them heading into dangerous territory; pray *with* them, and *for* them. And in doing so, you are truly *loving* them. And remember this: While the Holy Spirit convicts our hearts when necessary he never condemns: "There is **no condemnation <u>for those</u> who are in Christ Jesus**. For the law of the Spirit of life in Christ Jesus has set you **free** from the law of sin and of death" (Romans 1:8). The apostle Peter tells us that we are to "Above all, love one another deeply, because love covers a multitude of sin" (1 Peter 4:8). Jesus is the ultimate example, as it was because of His perfect love that He gave His own life as the covering for a multitude of sins, covering the sins of the entire world for as many as would receive Him. As Christians our most important job is to **love one another** in truth, to **share the message of salvation** through faith in Jesus to a lost world, and to **remind everyone of His imminent return** as it draws closer with each passing day.

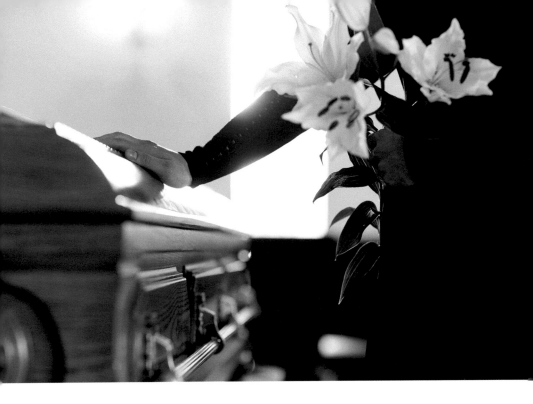

"We do not fix our eyes on what is seen, but what is unseen, since what is seen is temporary, but what is not seen is eternal."(2 Corinthians 4:18)

## *Chapter Ten*

### "YOU CAN'T TAKE IT WITH YOU"

B efore I get into some of the other various reasons that people have given for rejecting Christianity, I want to be sure to offer some caution about the deception that is in high gear during these last days, leading many astray in the name of Christianity. As I mentioned, if you attend a true Christian church, you will likely hear about sin and the grace of God, which covers the sin of mankind. On the other hand, for those who prefer **not** to hear about sin, I can assure you there are plenty of churches that go out of their way to avoid the subject of sin altogether. All you have to do is turn on your TV to find many of them. In order to please their audience and keep attendance up, many churches strictly adhere to *non-offensive*, uplifting, feel-good messages of success and prosperity. They don't guide their congregates through the scriptures to assist in their spiritual growth, and they rarely mention sin, or the redemptive blood of Jesus that was shed for their sins; they don't dare breathe a word about the wrath and judgment of God that belongs to those who reject God's offer. The messages from many pulpits these days are not addressing people's eternal destiny. Instead they're offering crowd-pleasing messages with a spiritual spin, using the Word of God as a template of principles on how to gain worldly success, making lighthearted quips out of biblical stories. They inject the name of Jesus as if it's a magic word to demand their own desires. Not all but many of these megachurch preachers will be sure to tell you all kinds of cool stuff that God can **do for you**: a better job, a promotion, a bigger house, a new or better relationship, freedom from sickness, or whatever it is you may be hoping for. But you won't hear them talking about what God **has already done** in sending His Son, Jesus, to die for you and why He did it. So many out there are nothing more than motivational speakers who finagle the scripture for their own purposes. The goal appears to be to keep people's heads buried in the sand, and their feet planted in the earth, rather than pointing them to eternity. They neglect the teaching of the most important *truth* that will carry them throughout this life and into the next. Instead they offer messages of how to achieve your best life here. They neglect the True Gospel: that Jesus died for the sins of mankind because we are all lost sinners and in need of a Savior, and that only through faith in Him, do we have eternal life. They neglect to mention that **without Jesus** there is **no eternal hope** for anyone, and even wrath and judgment are in store for those who reject this gospel once this life comes to a screeching halt. And it will. To leave this important information out of any sermon sounds like a dirty trick to me.

This brand of self-centered, world-centered preaching comes as no surprise to Christians who know the scriptures. We're warned to look out for *this very thing*. The apostle Paul warns that in the last days, "The time will come when many **within the church** will not endure sound doctrine; but rather, wanting to have their ears tickled, they will accumulate for themselves teachers in accordance to **their own desires**" (1 Timothy 4:3). You aren't likely to hear any of these prosperity preachers preach on *that* verse. These here-and-now preachers seem to want to keep people bound to the world, keeping their eyes on their worldly goals and aspirations, focused on the here and now. They are leading people astray while living the high life and lining their own pockets. They are neglecting the true gospel of Jesus, ignoring the obvious—that people are dying all around them and that this life here is *very temporary*, that we are **not** promised tomorrow. I feel it's vital to include the eternal message in any sermon, because the fact is we aren't promised tomorrow.

I found it interesting too that although many preachers are preaching humanistic messages, apparently they're in demand. Notice that the preceding verse tells us that many **within the church** are actually looking for these teachers who will tell them what they want to hear rather than the truth. A lot of folks want to go to a "cool" church, that plays "cool" music, and has a "cool" pastor who preaches a "cool" message. They want to be entertained and feel "spiritual" at the same time. So we have false preachers and *false followers too*, under the guise of Christianity. But those who belong to God, those who are steeped in His word, will know better. I've heard that people who are trained to spot counterfeit money are trained by familiarizing themselves with and studying the distinct characteristics of the *real* bills, so when they come across a counterfeit, they will easily recognize it as a *fake*. Although the fake bill will have many of the same characteristics, enough to fool many, those who know what to look for won't be fooled by it. The same goes for those who know the word of God: they will see the deception for what it is.

Anyway, I'm all for success and prosperity, and I enjoy a good, uplifting message too. Who doesn't? Christians are often accused of being "negative." Although the message of truth is what everyone needs to hear, it may not be what they want to hear, and it is anything BUT negative! Many years before writing this book, I had written a short message explaining the Gospel. I kept copies of it wherever I'd go. I would give it to people I knew and people I met, in order to try to share God's gift of eternal life through grace. In short, the message explained that we're all going to die one day, (which I figured was no big secret) and that the good news is Jesus! I heard through the proverbial grapevine that someone I had given it to, referred to it as "Nancy's death paper." I didn't know whether to laugh or cry. Instead, I just prayed for them more. Clearly they missed the point or more likely they simply weren't interested in it. The common expression used today: "It's all good," perfectly describes the message that Christians so desperately want to share with people; that's because they understand mankind's eternal destination without it. They understand that *eternity* is a very long time.

*The Gospel* actually means "The Good News," and it is *very good news*, very uplifting when you consider the reality of *the bad news*: that we're all going to die one day. There's just no way around that. What could be better news than to hear that because of what Jesus has done on our behalf, death isn't the end of your life but the beginning of your eternal life? Now that's some really good news! The Gospel of Christ gives us *eternal* hope; we can rest easy knowing that Jesus has settled the matter for us personally. Knowing that our eternity is settled, we can enjoy our life here so much more, because we have the proper perspective giving us "the peace of God that surpasses all understanding" (Philippians 4:7). Christians don't need to go through life worrying about death. Remember, we know the ending of our story: it ends with an astounding *happily **ever** after!* In the big picture, we all know the old adage; "You can't take it with you," whether we're talking about our booming business, our beautiful home, our expensive jewelry, our new sports car, or our awards and trophies. If your main goal and focus is to have your best life here, then that will be your *big* reward!

Christians understand that as much as we enjoy and appreciate the blessings God has bestowed upon us, whether it be our homes, our families, our special talents, our status or position, or whatever, those things are *not the main focus* in life. Those things are all temporal pleasures and can end in a literal heartbeat. We understand that we can enjoy and appreciate the blessings, but we don't cling too tightly. We're living and enjoying our lives with an eternal focus, which helps us to live with the proper perspective while we're here on earth, whatever our circumstances. We understand that all of our worldly success, status, and prosperity or whatever it may be, will only go so far, and will mean absolutely nothing going into eternity. We're reminded of this throughout the scriptures. "Love **not the world**, neither the things that are in the world. If any man loves the world, the love of the Father

**is not** in him" (1 John 2:15). "We **do not** fix our eyes on what is seen, but what is **unseen**, since what is seen is **temporary**, but what is not seen is **eternal**" (2 Corinthians 4:18). "If then you have been made new in Christ, seek the things that are above, where Christ is seated at the right hand of God the Father. **Set your minds on things that are above, not on things of the earth**" (Colossians 3:2). "**Do not** lay up for yourselves treasures **on earth**, where moth and rust destroy and where thieves break in and steal, but instead **lay up for yourselves treasures in heaven**, where neither moth nor rust destroys and where thieves do not break in and steal" (Matthew 6:1).

I hate to imagine the multitudes of people standing at the gates of heaven before the God who created heaven and earth and all its bounty, holding out their portfolios, waving their worldly credentials and accolades at Him: "I am the richest man in the world!" "I've been an outstanding citizen in my community." "I took good care of the environment." "I am the CEO of the largest company in the world." "I have the world's most impressive car collection." "I've won five Oscars." "I was inducted into the Rock and Roll Hall of Fame." "I've faithfully attended church my whole life." "I've given more to charitable donations than anyone in the world!" "I've been a 'really good' person." "I spent my life fighting for social justice." "I won the Nobel Peace Prize!" "I found the cure for cancer and invented a lifesaving vaccine!"

While those things may be very impressive to most people, they won't impress God in the least. Why would they? God is well aware that we couldn't have been anything or done anything *at all* without *Him*! "For *by Him* were all things created, that are in heaven and that are in the earth, visible and invisible, whether they be thrones, or dominions, or principalities, or powers: all things were created *by Him and for Him*. And He is before all things, and *by Him* do all things exist" (Colossians 1:16). "Every good gift, every perfect gift comes down *from the Father* of lights" (James 1:17). "*Apart from Me*, you can do nothing" (John 15:15). "It is *because of Him* that we live and move and breathe" (Acts 17:28). *That* is the God we will stand before at the gates of heaven! It's important to have the proper perspective. If you show up at His gates, the *one and only* credential He will be looking for on that day will be *your faith in Jesus*, His only begotten Son, whom He personally sent to save you, to pay the debt that you owed. When the apostles asked Jesus what God required of them to enter His Kingdom, He answered, "The work of God is this: *to believe in the One* He has sent" (John 6:29). The apostle John said, "This is His command: *to believe* in the Name of His Son, Jesus Christ" (1 John 3:23). Jesus said, "He who does not believe is condemned already because he has *not believed* in the name of the only begotten Son of God " (John 3:18). For those who show up without that one and only credential, God will say to them: "Depart from me, I never knew you..." (Psalm 119:115, Matthew 7:23, Luke 13:27).

"But the Spirit explicitly says that in later times **some will fall away** from the faith, paying attention to deceitful spirits and doctrines of demons." (1 Timothy 4:1)

## Chapter Eleven

## TOLERANCE

Another deception and very popular these days are the all-inclusive churches where there is no moral standard to speak of. Basically it's anything goes. The truth of God's word, is anything *but* anything goes, and apparently it has become very offensive in today's culture. Many churches today might just as well have thrown the Bible out the window. They preach what I call, the gospel of tolerance. Which wouldn't bother me at all if they didn't call themselves Christians. God's word has another name for them: evil *imposters*, who go from bad to worse, deceiving and being deceived. (2 Timothy 3:8-13) As I mentioned, these days people are more comfortable with terms such as "my truth" or "your truth" because it's less offensive to them than **God's truth**. The truth of God's word has become unacceptable and unpalatable these days. It's considered outdated, irrelevant and backward; "it's so negative, it's a real downer." This comes as no surprise to God and no surprise to those who have held tightly to the word of God. Over the past several decades, many churches are only referencing the Bible verses that fit their message and standard of *tolerance*: taking bible verses out of context, preaching superficial topical messages about love. But what is love without truth? These churches ignore or throw out any verses that they consider to be offensive for the new "woke" generation. They've replaced the truth with tolerance, which is far more appealing to the masses. It's all the rage these days. Everyone's got to be "tolerant." Yet strangely enough these same groups professing to be so tolerant, inclusive, and accepting have no tolerance for those who hold fast to all of the fundamental, historical biblical beliefs— the moral standards set forth by God. They're conforming the word of God to fit the culture instead of transforming the culture through the word of God. This new movement has absolutely no tolerance for conservative Bible believing Christians. Apparently that's where their tolerance ends. Those who cling to the classical beliefs from the Bible are mocked, called judgmental, stupid, backward, and even hateful. Beyond that, these days it seems even being tolerant isn't enough. We're expected to embrace whatever new trend comes along, even to celebrate it and join the parade. To be considered "loving and tolerant" these days we all must accept and applaud the new standard each time the bar is lowered. It's as if someone redefined the word *tolerant*!

Christians are not perfect, and I'm living proof of that. But none that I know are backward, hateful, or intolerant. My intention throughout my life has always been to be loving and kind to anyone I encounter regardless of their lifestyle choices. I can, and do tolerate many behaviors that I may feel are personally unacceptable or morally wrong. However, the fact that I may not go along with, agree with, or refuse to endorse a particular behavior or group, doesn't mean that I am hateful or intolerant. The very word *tolerant* indicates that there is a disagreement or a difference of opinion. According to the dictionary, to tolerate means to "put up with." Everyone can choose to *put up with* a particular event, behavior, or group in spite of how they may feel about it personally. And although they may *tolerate* something, that doesn't mean that they shouldn't have the right to reject it, or kindly express their opinions or feelings about it without being called hateful. Using Jesus as our example, we should love the sinner, but hate the sin. And there are times when we may need to love them enough to tell them the truth.

This is the thing: whether we're comfortable with the standards or not, there are various behaviors and actions that are without question, considered wrong, sinful, unacceptable even intolerable *according to God's word.* So don't shoot the messengers. Biblically speaking there may be some *grey areas* when it comes to sin, but most are *plain as day areas.* As Christians we should *want* to know those things that are unacceptable according to God, and do our best to avoid them. We should also be prepared to take a stand *against them* when necessary. God's word is our steady standard; it doesn't bend and change with the laws or the culture. Understanding this may require some self-reflection, a change of attitude, a change of heart, a cry for forgiveness, even in areas where we ourselves may have fallen in the past, as well as in present areas of our lives. "If we confess our sins, He is faithful and just to forgive us and cleanse us from all unrighteousness." (1 John 1:9) My point is this: while Christians may not always live up to the biblical values and standards set forth by God; if we say we are Christians, it should be *our desire* to learn about them, to *want* to live by them, and we should not be ashamed or afraid to stand up *for them.* And most importantly, we fully understand that Jesus is our only covering when we fall short of them. "For you were once children of darkness, **but now** you are light in the Lord. So walk as children of the light. **Seeking out** what is **acceptable to the Lord**" (Ephesians 5:8).

*"Follow me, and I will make you fishers of men." (Matthew 4:19)*

## Chapter Twelve

## MAKING THE WORLD A BETTER PLACE

Another subtle deception has crept into many, even previously conservative, evangelical churches in these last days; they have turned their attentions to a new *social justice gospel* as they join together to make the world a better place. This may come as a surprise or even an offense to many, but the **True Gospel** of Christ has little, if anything to do with making this world a better place or issues of *social justice*. Although those things may be a result of it to some degree, it is **not the purpose** of the True Gospel of Jesus. Jesus said to His followers as He hand-selected them, things such as this: "Follow me, and I will make you fishers of men" (Matthew. 4:19, Mark 1:17). Jesus was interested in the *repentance* from sin and the *salvation* of **the individual soul** from *eternal damnation*. You won't find Jesus saying anything like this:

"Follow me and we'll make the world a better place." "Follow me and we'll save the planet." Neither did Jesus say "Follow me and we'll make sure that everything is 'Even Steven, fair and square.'" There is no suggestion throughout the New Testament that our mission as followers of Jesus was to "make the world a better place or fight for social equality." However, this humanistic, social-justice gospel has mass appeal and is very subtle and misleading, because everyone wants to make the world a better place. Right?

In short, the purpose of the true gospel as preached by the apostles is to point people to their *personal need* for forgiveness and ultimately to eternity. The gospel of Christ is this: Jesus died on the cross for our sins, shedding His own blood, paying the debt we owed, and He is offering salvation and eternal life to everyone who accepts that and believes; there is **no other name** given under heaven whereby man must be saved. And the whole point in knowing that, is to share this good news with everyone you can; we are to do this *for the very reason* that this world is **not** going to be here forever, **nor will they!** Everyone seems to be missing the point with this new social-justice gospel. The same goes for the gospel of dominionism or kingdom theology, as well as the group known as the New Apostolic Reformation, and others, all having more or less the same message: that Christians are here to make the world a better place and get it ready for the arrival of Jesus. Really? These are by no means biblical views. Just more of Satan's deception that has crept into the church. Speaking of "a better place," Jesus said that it will be *in His Father's house*: "I am going *there* to prepare a place for you. And if I go and prepare a place for you, I will come back and *take you to be with me*" (John 14:3). Jesus made it very clear: "My Kingdom is **NOT** *of this world*" (John 18:36). In no way does this next passage suggest that we shouldn't do our own part to help the poor, but Jesus tells us "The poor you will always have with you." (Matthew 26:11) He also said, "*This world* is passing away" (1 Corinthians 7:31). We are to have our hearts and minds set on "things above, **not** *on the things of the earth.*"(Colossians 3:1-2)

Of course, Christians should all do their own part to make this world a better place while we're here: through our own repentance and salvation with the help of the Holy Spirit of God, we should be the salt and light of the world using Jesus as our example, feeding the poor in as much as we're able as we're led by the spirit of God, and according to the apostle, Paul, foremostly when it comes to our Christian brothers and sisters. We should be helping our neighbors, being kind to everyone we encounter, living out a high moral standard, and so on. The purpose for doing all of these things, is that by our example, we will bring others to a saving knowledge of God's grace through faith in His only begotten Son, Jesus. Naturally we should also do our best to take care of our environment while we're here, but keeping the proper biblical perspective: that the earth is here to serve us, not the other way around. As Christians we're *not* here to fix the world's social, environmental, and economic problems. Satan is the master deceiver. What better place to infiltrate his deception than in a Christian church.

There is no scriptural foundations for these teachings. There is *absolutely no promise* from God that this world as a whole is ever going to be "a better place," because it is hopelessly infected with sin. In fact the Bible tells us the opposite: we know from the scriptures that the world will only get worse and worse until Jesus returns to judge it and all those who have rejected Him. We're also told to look for the signs of His coming, and by the looks of things, that time is rapidly approaching. That is the urgent message that the world needs to hear. But it seems that many churches have been deceived, distracted, and diverted by all kinds of new gospels, each with an entirely different cause and message, and it's spreading like wildfire. "But even if we or even an angel from heaven should preach a gospel other than the one we preached to you, let them be under God's curse!" (Galatians 1:8). So I caution you: don't be fooled by a counterfeit bill of goods.

*"He has made from **one blood** every nation of men to dwell on all the face of the earth, and has determined their preappointed times and the boundaries of their dwellings." (Acts 17:26)*

## Chapter Thirteen

### ALL LIVES MATTER TO GOD

I was reluctant to bring this up because of its controversial nature. But I've been led to do so anyway. As with the previous cautions of deception, I am speaking to those who are interested in the *biblical* view of all things. There is another evil, deceptive ideology sweeping across the globe, and sadly, it has recently even been embraced by many naive Christians and church leaders who, perhaps well intended themselves, haven't taken the time to investigate the intentions and doctrines of this group; they want to be sure not to be considered insensitive or a racist. This divisive ideology comes from the organization Black Lives Matter. In short, the organization promotes a view of "oppressors" and "oppressed" between races. It's sparking great division through a false and, more importantly for Christians to realize, an *unbiblical* narrative, claiming one particular group as victims of another's generations of transgressions. Most would agree wholeheartedly with the statement

"Black lives matter." No one can sanely argue with that statement. But the fact is that *all* **lives matter**. Yet a statement like that is considered to be racist to promoters and members of this radical organization. Their ideology of oppressors and oppressed is nothing new; it's just good-old-fashioned Marxism repackaged for this generation of the last days. Sadly many beloved Christian pastors, authors, and teachers have been deceived and fallen for this dangerous and deceptive ideology, publicly bowing down in submission to—and apologizing for—accusations of the various offenses of history, giving in to the demands of those propagating it.

Biblically speaking, the only thing that any Christian should be bowing down to is the *cross of Jesus*. This group's ideology stems from something being widely taught, known as Critical Race Theory, and it has indoctrinated many; it is unbiblical at best and demonic at worst. The important thing to recognize is that there is only **one race** to consider: the *human race*. "He has made from **one blood** every nation of men to dwell on all the face of the earth, and has determined their pre-appointed times and the boundaries of their dwellings." (Acts 17:26) I learned this simple truth as a child, from the well-known childrens's song, Jesus Loves the Little Children; the most popular line goes like this: "Red, brown, yellow, black and white, they're *all* precious in God's sight." Biblically speaking, we are each *individually* responsible and accountable for our own actions: accountable to God personally and also to our fellow man for how we *personally* treat one another. However, each of us as individuals are *not responsible* for the particular, specific, personal transgressions of any previous group, generation or person; the **only** thing passed down to us as the human race is our *own personal* spiritual DNA of sin. With that, Jesus is the answer for all— every *race, tribe, and tongue*. I won't take the time to dissect each of this group's mission statements; however, I will say that every single facet of this group's ideology goes against the very core of Christianity and in fact against God Himself. It is *all* **Anti-Christ**. Yet people everywhere are being deceived by this group or bullied into going along with it, for fear of being called a racist. "But the Spirit of God explicitly says that in later times **some will fall away** from the faith, paying attention to *deceitful spirits* and *doctrines of demons*" (1 Timothy 4:1). They are the great pretenders, imposters. "They went out from us, but they did not *really* belong to us. For if they had belonged to us, they would have remained with us; but their going *showed that none of them* belonged to us." (1 John 2:19) None of this is a surprise to God. He knew it would happen at the end of the age and He let us know too.

"For God has *not* given us the spirit of fear; but of **power**, and of **love**, and of a **sound mind**."(2 Timothy 1:7)

## *Chapter Fourteen*

# HEY, WHERE'D YOU GET THAT STUPID HAT?

Okay, back to some of the reasons that people may reject Christianity. Fear can be a factor that may keep some from coming to Christ. People may be afraid of what other people will think of them. They're afraid of being mocked, whispered about, made the butt of the joke, left out, or persecuted in some way, and they fear they will be referred to as a religious nut or a Jesus freak. I understand and relate to all of those things. People might be afraid and worry that they'll lose their friends or their husband, or even their job, at the mention of Jesus. **Well, they may.** Jesus Himself gave us a warning of this very thing: "If the world hates you, remember it hated me first" (John 15:18). Jesus also warned that following Him may even cause division among families: "They will be divided, father against son, and son against father, mother against daughter and daughter against mother" (Luke 25:53, Matthew 10:34-35). So I won't mislead you by telling you that if you place your faith in Jesus, your life will be trouble-free, because I can assure you it won't. Although the gift of salvation and eternal life is absolutely free, it comes with a personal cost. I'll explain it like this just for practical purposes: Let's say that someone offers you a free hat. It's a **really great hat**; it adjusts to your own body temperature, it's waterproof, it glows in the dark, it has high-tech sensors that warn you of various threats, it will even cause hair growth for thinning hair, and so on. Wow, and this great hat is *100 percent free and it is available to **everyone** who wants one*! However, there may be people—even people in your own family—who will make fun of you for wearing it. *That* would be the "personal cost" of wearing your free hat regardless of the amazing benefits of wearing it.

It's especially true in this day and age that Christians everywhere are looked down upon, mocked, ridiculed, and marginalized—and in many countries, even put to death—for their faith in Jesus. And it's getting worse right here in America of all places. A recent article in the L.A. Times from January, 2021 labeled Bible believing Christians as "White Nationalists" expressing that they should not be allowed to run for any public office, suggesting that they should be reprogrammed or weeded out of society all together. According to the article, apparently whether you're black, white or anything in between, if you're a Bible believing Christian you're considered a White Nationalist. They seem to have forgotten that Jesus, who we follow was a Jew from the Middle East. Also in January 2021 a letter from a group of Democratic Congressmen and women from across the U.S. was sent to the new administration echoing the same message. It was a call for a *Secular America*. The letter demands that Conservative, evangelical Bible believing Christians and everything they represent should be ousted from every area of society; referring to their biblical beliefs as a danger and a threat to all others. The letter included a long list of changes that need to take place including removing the words "In God we trust" from dollar bills and to avoid using the term "Judeo-Christian values."

I find it interesting that they are so desperate to remove God from every aspect of society. The evil principalities and spiritual forces of darkness are really threatened. However, they aren't the least bit worried about the liberal, "all inclusive," churches and pastors because they've got *them* in their grips.

Anyway, this is what you're up against if you're a follower of Jesus these days, right here in what was once considered the land of the free. "We're not in Kansas anymore!" Yes, now more than ever during these last days, there is a personal cost for standing up for your beliefs if you're a true Christian. But nothing we will **ever** endure can compare to what it cost Jesus, who paid the ultimate price to save mankind. Remember that our fear will not change the truth, and the truth will set you free. Although Christians, myself included, may even be guilty of being *too tolerant* at times and may not always be as brave or bold as we should be when it comes to sharing our faith; I don't know a single Christian who would abandon his or her faith in spite of the persecution that may come with it. In fact the apostle James said to "count it all joy!" (James 1:2–8). With the world in its current condition, we have a lot of joy ahead of us by way of persecution. The apostle Matthew tells us how we should respond to persecution for our faith: "Rejoice and be glad for your reward is great in Heaven" (Matthew 5:12). Jesus offered these words of encouragement: "In the world there will be tribulations but take courage, I have overcome the world!" (John 16:33). Jesus makes it very clear that walking with Him is **not** a walk in the park. That's why He said, "If anyone wants to follow me, take up your cross and follow" (Matthew 16:24). The apostle Luke tells us, "It is through many tribulations that we enter the Kingdom of God" (Acts 14:22). We understand through scripture that we will face all kinds of troubles, obstacles, ridicule, rejection and persecution when it comes to our faith in Jesus, even from people you'd never expect. You may find that people aren't interested in your message or in your company anymore, and although it may hurt, we have constant comfort from God, He can fill the void of any loss with truth and joy. "There is no fear in love, but perfect love casts out fear" (1 John 4:18). "In God I trust and I am not afraid. What can *mere mortals* do to me?" (Psalms 56:1–8) We have the Spirit of God living within us. "Greater is He Who is in me than he that is in the world" (1 John 4:4). God's power is *second to* *none*, and though we have battles in this life to conquer, God has won the war! "If God is for me who can stand against me?" (Romans 8:31). I am under His constant protection, and I am shielded by the "full armor of God" as I go through each day. (Ephesians 6:10). God will calm your spirit and give you strength through everything life throws at you. Although I have trials and sorrows abounding daily, and by the looks of things, more to come, God's love will never fail me. "Do not fear for I am with you, for I am your God. I will strengthen you and help you; I will uphold you with my righteous hand" (Isaiah 4:10). Christians serve a *risen, living* God. The apostle Paul tells us, "For God has **not** given us the spirit of fear; but of *power, and of love,* and of a <u>*sound mind*</u>" (2 Timothy 1:7). Life looks very different as we look through the lens of eternity. This lens gives us the proper perspective and insight even as we face the events taking place in the world today. Christians have God's word as their ultimate source of truth.

Viewing life through the eyes of God alters the way we see *everything*, even removing the fear of tragedy and death. This was the way the apostle Paul felt about his own death: "We are confident, I say, and *prefer* rather to be absent from the body and to be present with the Lord" (2 Corinthians 5:8). He tells us also, "To live, is [to live for] Christ, but *to die is gain*" (Philippians 1:21). The apostle Paul confesses he was torn between life and death as he understood clearly his purpose here was to bring others to a saving knowledge of Christ: "However, I consider my life worth nothing to me; my only aim is to finish the race and complete the task the Lord Jesus has given me—the task of testifying to the *good news* of God's grace. I am torn between the two. I desire to depart and be with Christ, which is *far better indeed*" (Acts 20:24). Not only did the death and resurrection of Jesus accomplished many things, the writer of the book of Hebrews tells us that His death was in part, to *free mankind from the fear of death.* (Hebrews 2: 14-15).

Do you see the theme here? Even death is nothing to fear if you are a Christian. As Christians, we all have lives to live, jobs to do, and a purpose to fulfill while we're here, but we have no need to worry about or fear death. When our time comes, we will instantly enter into something **so** far superior than anything we can imagine or have ever experienced before. The Creator, the Grand Designer of the Universe, holds me gently in His hands through all of my troubles and will safely bring me home at *His appointed time* and not a minute sooner, regardless of anything. God is always **on** my side and **by** my side, and He is the very essence of love, so I have nothing to fear. God didn't promise us that it will be easy to follow Him but that it will be *well* worth it. "I consider that our present sufferings are not worthy of being compared with the glory that will be revealed to us" (2 Corinthians 4:17, 2 Timothy 2:10). These promises belong to me, and to all who place their faith in Jesus. So go ahead and rock that free hat fearlessly!

"Do you want to be made well?" (John 5:6)

## *Chapter Fifteen*

## WE'RE ONLY HUMAN

**P**ride is another obstacle, and I believe, the biggest one to overcome. While knowing that *we are all sinners*, Jesus said, "It is not the healthy who need a doctor but the sick. I have not come to call the righteous but sinners" (Luke 5:31). But before anyone can say "Oh good; I don't need a doctor," (or a Savior) we're soon reminded, "If we say we have no sin, we deceive ourselves and *the truth* is not in us" (1 John 1:18). The word **sin** comes from an archery term and simply means "*missing the mark*," but people don't like to think of themselves as sinners. People who know me know that I'm one of those people who is very stubborn when it comes to going to a doctor. But eventually when I get so sick of being sick, I'll finally admit that I need a doctor.

This story about Jesus healing the lame man by the healing pool in Jerusalem comes to my mind: Jesus came across a lame man sitting alongside the pool. This poor man had been lame for his entire life. Jesus walked up to him and asked, "Do you want to be made well?" (John 5:6). It seems like an odd question to ask a lame man. You'd think, *Of course he wants to be made well! He was born lame and has never walked a day in his life!* The man responded by telling Jesus that he had no one to help him into the pool and so on. Jesus said to him, "Rise, take up your bed and walk" (John 5:8–9). Just like that, the man was healed. Beyond that, he had the appropriate response. He was so thankful, that he ran jumping for joy throughout the city, telling people about what Jesus had done for him. That man **wanted** to be made well. However, throughout my life, I've found that many people don't really want to be made well. Have you ever tried to help a home-less person get off the streets or a drug addict get into a drug program? I have many times, from family members to random people sitting by their shopping carts on the streets. I've found that most will take your money but will refuse any *real help* because they're not ready to change their lives; they're actually comfortable right where they are and will be the first to tell you that they're fine.

When it comes to being made spiritually well, most people are like that. They highly esteem themselves or their life is going along pretty well, so they don't see any need for a Savior, because as they see it, they're just fine. They don't feel any need for forgiveness: *Who me, what did I do?* After all, they're not that guilty guy sitting on death row; they're "not *that* bad" or they're "good *enough*." Comparatively speaking, by their own standards, they may evaluate themselves as "better than most" or even consider themselves to be a "really good person." Most people have little or no interest in God; they simply don't think they need His forgiveness, because they're completely con-fident in their own wonderfulness. The more "together" they are, the less they think they need God. They may look at a homeless person or an addict and say, "Well, it's obvious that those people need help, but me? No. I'm doing all right. Right?" They have built the perfect life for themselves, and things are going along according to their plans; "first comes love, then comes marriage, then comes the baby in the baby car-riage," or whatever their plans may be. But to God who's looking at their heart and their eternal condition, they're still sitting on the corner with their shopping cart, broke, filthy, hungry, and in desperate need of help.

That's why pride stands in the way for so many, because those accepting God's gift of salvation must recognize their own need for forgiveness, which takes a *humble* heart. They need to accept that without **Jesus**, all of their own goodness or perfectly laid plans, **will not meet** the one and **only** requirement to enter heaven; it will be kind of like showing up for a job interview with an amazing résumé, but you don't have the passcode to get into the building where the interview is to be held. Your amazing résumé will be of no help to you *without* that all-important passcode. *Jesus* is the **only** passcode that will get you into heaven. "There is *no other name given* under heaven where by man must be saved" (Acts 4:12).

We know that any way you look at it, "not that bad," "pretty good," and even "better than most" aren't perfect. It's a fact that "nobody's perfect." God has placed that truth in our hearts, and His standards are sealed in our consciences. We have all missed the mark of perfection. However, God being God requires perfection according to **His** standards to enter into heaven, **not ours**; perfect in every thought, every motive, every word, every action, every minute of every day, every single day of our lives. And you wouldn't expect anything less from God, but it's a tall order for us. After all, we're only human. Thankfully God is not, and He's got us covered if only we ask. "God opposes the proud, but gives grace to the humble" (James 4:6). "Humble yourself in the sight of the Lord, and He will lift you up" (James 4:10). "Pride goeth before destruction and a haughty spirit before a fall" (Proverbs 16:18). "The loftiness of man shall be humbled. The haughtiness of men shall be brought down and the Lord shall be exalted in that day" (Isaiah 2:11–12).

"As the heavens are higher than the earth, My ways are higher than your ways and My thoughts, than your thoughts." (Isaiah 55:9)

## Chapter Sixteen

## A WAY THAT *SEEMS* RIGHT TO A MAN

We all see the world around us changing rapidly and evolving before our eyes to the point that *morality has become subjective*. The human race today either denies the existence of God or they assume that God has changed, or should have changed His standards to accommodate the changing world with its "Anything goes," "If it feels good, do it" morality. Much like the moral conditions described in the Old Testament marking the beginning of the collapse of the Nation of Israel. We're told that during that time there was no king and "each man did what was right in *their own* eyes" (Judges. 21:25). The Book of Proverbs tells us "There is a way that *seems right* to a man, but the end *leads to death*" (Proverbs 4:12). God's standards are not subject to our opinions. God's standards are not subject to anyone. He is God: "As the heavens are higher than the earth, My ways are higher than your ways and my thoughts, than your thoughts" (Isaiah 55:9). His laws and standards have been *preordained* from eternity. Although the world is rapidly changing, "God is the same yesterday, today and forever" (Hebrews 13:8). Although the times are changing, **God has not.** God has revealed Himself to us through His Word: both the incarnate Word, Jesus, "the Word [who] became flesh and dwelt among us," (John 1:14) as well as His written Word. He has generously imparted His standards to mankind throughout various periods in history in order to fulfill *His purpose for our good.* Ultimately God knows what's best for us. After all, He is the Grand Designer of the Universe and everything in it! God knows exactly how He designed mankind, and He knows how He designed the world to operate in order to achieve optimal and perfect results. God isn't required to bend His will to align with ours. God isn't required to amend His standards to satisfy the desires or whims of mankind or with the changing of the times, cultures and civilizations. He would hardly be worthy of being called God if that were the case. So here again the dilemma: God's standard of perfection is still required to enter heaven, yet according to God, "Nobody's perfect." God hasn't changed His mind about what's right and wrong or good and evil or what's acceptable behavior and what is not. Just like a loving parent, God has set His limitations and His standards for our benefit, because of His love for us and because He knows what's best for us. God hasn't said, "Well, you know, everyone's doing it; I really need to be more progressive, tolerant, and inclusive in order to avoid a big protest, so I'll just go ahead and lower My standards." God does not capitulate or lower His standards, and God being God isn't swayed by temper tantrums or protests. And there's no doubt in my mind that God is deeply aggrieved by some of the things He sees going on in the world today and the rapid downshift of long-standing moral standards. But God being God is full of mercy and knows our struggle; He knows what we're going through and he understands the pressures we face in this fallen world. God understands and realizes "The spirit is willing but the flesh is weak" (Matthew 26:41). But He loves us so much that He has made a perfect plan for us in the midst of a fallen and sinful world. But it is up to each individually to accept or reject His offer.

Some people look at the condition of the world—whether wars, murders, addiction, floods, earthquakes, economic collapse, a world-wide virus, riots, or whatever may come next; still they somehow have the idea that all the problems of the planet can be solved and overcome by the goodness of mankind. As much as I appreciate such an optimistic outlook, all I can say is, "How's that been working so far?" The very idea that the goodness of mankind can bring about peace or defeat the turmoil in the world is not without problems. First of all, everyone has to *agree* on what's good. That has not yet happened throughout the history of mankind. Each person or group has very different ideas about what's good and which direction is the right direction to go, what is the right thing to do, and so forth. Each one is tainted by their own sinful nature and motivated by various inclinations, whether it be power, personal ambition, religion, greed, or whatever personally drives them, sending each in different directions. In other words, one man's "goodness" is another man's "evil." The word of God tells us "The heart [of man] is deceitful above all things and desperately wicked."(-Jeremiah 17:9). So we continue to fool ourselves. Consider too, the spiritual warfare and the agenda of Satan. All you have to do is open a history book or turn on the local news to see that the goodness of mankind simply isn't enough to cure the problems of the world. It would require continuous acts of goodness 24 hours a day, 365 days a year from every single person on the planet. Oh, right, and they'd all have to *agree* on what goodness is.

This is not to say that there haven't been many acts of what most consider goodness, heroism, and kindness throughout history; we have all read about them or personally witnessed them. And we continue to witness and even take part in what we may consider acts of kindness every day, but even with that, here we are in a world that is looking bleaker by the minute. Mankind can't seem to agree on what's good for the world. They can't seem to agree on anything. The fact is we are living in a fallen world with fallen, imperfect people. It seems obvious to me that without an absolute **truth**, there will never be peace in this world. We know that mankind doesn't deal well with absolutes by the way they respond to the idea of God as an absolute authority.

Thankfully though, we know through the scriptures that in the not-so-distant future, God **will** be the absolute authority. We will live in His perfect kingdom, and rule with Him there. Ultimately our true home and eternal destiny is a place where each citizen has been hand-selected by God. Those who called upon His name to save them, will be in perfect harmony with Him and with each other; there will be no division, and there will be *unending* peace and joy throughout the eternal Kingdom of God. Heaven is a real place and the eternal destination of those who have placed their faith in Jesus. In fact Jesus said that He's going to prepare a place for us up there: "In My Father's house there are many mansions. I go to prepare a place for you that where I am you may be too" (John 14:3). People are usually hearing those words as they stand at the gravesite of a loved one. But I never hear any talk about the truth of those words or see any indication that people actually *believe* them once the service is over. But I, along with millions of others, **do** believe them. We can take those words to the bank and cash them in for an eternity of wonders because they were spoken by the resurrected, *living Savior* of the world: God Himself. "Since you have been raised to new life in Christ, *set your hearts on things above* where Christ is seated at the right hand of God, the Father. So, set your minds on things above, *not on earthly things*" (Colossians 3:1–52).

"No eye has seen, no ear has heard, no mind can imagine the things that God has prepared for those who love Him. (1 Corinthians 13:12)

## Chapter Seventeen

### IMAGINE *THAT!*

I've found my treasure in Jesus. He has given me eternal life! "Where your treasure is, there your heart will be also" (Matthew 6:21). My heart and mind are firmly set on the things above. I have confidence that by the time I reach the Kingdom of God, my place will be all ready for me. I'm thinking back to a couple years ago when my Aunt Carol and Uncle Jim were coming to visit from Florida for my mother's big ninetieth birthday party. I was so excited to have them staying at our home. I wanted to make our home, and especially the guest room where they'd be staying, extra-special, paying attention to every detail, thinking of things that would make them feel comfortable and at home while they were here. My husband mounted a flat-screen TV in their room so they could watch their favorite shows in bed if they liked, I got new bedding and hung new curtains, put fresh flowers on the make-up table, and so on. As I think of that visit and my own *menial* preparations, I can only imagine what kind of personal touches and special efforts Jesus, who knows each of our heart's desires, has gone to in His preparations *for us.* It will be a glorious sight to see, and I can hardly wait. Those who have placed their faith in Jesus already know the wonders of God, each from their own personal experiences with Him, through His word, through nature and creation, and through their own journey of faith, and we already have a glimpse of heaven.

However, by the time we actually arrive, we will have also seen the magnificence and greatness of the Lord God up close and personal; we will have witnessed from a place of safety the events of the great tribulation. We will have a better understanding of God's ultimate and infinite power and His perfect justice. By then we will have been resurrected ourselves and clothed in our new eternal bodies! At that time, each citizen will have a fuller appreciation of the majesty and awesomeness of God, and I can only imagine that we will be in complete awe of Him because we will be in His presence, "we will see Him face to face" (1 John 3:2). We are told that "we will be like Him as we will see Him as He is" (1 Corinthians 13:12). We will marvel at everything He is and everything He has done. We will have a fuller and deeper understanding of the magnitude of God's sacrifice for us when we see Him. We will finally have the validation of our own faith, and we will feel a deeper sense of gratitude, *far beyond* what we feel now as we look forward to our arrival. Beyond that, and far better too, we will see the *vindication of our Lord and Savior, Jesus,* who was publicly humiliated and denigrated before mankind; He was falsely charged and sentenced to death with the help of an angry mob, violently and brutally tortured, spit on, mocked, and scoffed at, he had hairs yanked from His beard. He was beaten and bludgeoned beyond recognition, crowned with a wreath of thorns, forced to carry His own implement of death, nailed to a cross, pierced with a sword, and left to hang there in agony, gasping for breath till He was dead. He asked only one thing through it all; He asked His Father to forgive those who had done this to Him. Jesus will also be vindicated for the centuries since His death and resurrection, during which He's been doubted, mocked, laughed about, ignored, dismissed, denied, and rebelled against; had His name used in vain and in curses of anger; and been the butt of many jokes. After all He's endured, it will be a wonderful day when we see Jesus sitting in His rightful place of power, in all His glory and majesty. It will be a day of rejoicing that I look forward to with great anticipation. As I think of Jesus and of all the torture and suffering I just described, it is yet another thing beyond my comprehension to realize that He was born for this very purpose: to pay a debt that we couldn't pay for ourselves. He gave His life willingly, "as a ransom for many" (Mark 10:45). He knew all of this was going to happen to Him and could have stopped it at any time. He could have said as His time drew closer, and with each strike of the whip, "I changed my mind," and poof, He would have been back in the comforts of heaven with His Father. But He didn't. He knew what had to be done in order to save us. Jesus said, "No one can take my life. I lay it down freely and have authority to take it up again" (John 10:18). And that's just what He did. That just blows my mind.

We all may try to imagine from time to time what it may be like to see God, the God that the Bible speaks of—a God who brought the entire universe into existence with His Word; a God who can lift and hold up the waters of the sea to make a path of escape for His people; a God who knows all things, sees all things, and can do all things; a God whose love is so extreme that He willingly came down from heaven, became flesh, endured intense humiliation, and gave His own life for us so that we may live eternally with *Him*. It's mind-bending to even try to imagine what it will be like. But at that time, all these things we have taken in faith up till then will be fully revealed to us. And no doubt we will be humbled and amazed. Nowadays we use the word *awesome* very frivolously: "My car is awesome," "Your hair looks awesome," "This burger is awesome," "The concert was awesome." When we get to heaven, these things will pale in comparison because we will know the true meaning of the word *awesome*!

I was thinking the other day about John Lennon's most famous song, "Imagine." The song was an instant hit and a welcome addition to the Eastern philosophies of the new age of enlightenment that was beginning to bloom back then. He starts off by saying "Imagine there's no heaven, Imagine there's no hell . . . Imagine all the people living for today." It sounds soothing and enlightening, almost transcendental, lulling people into thinking that if only they imagine and all sing kumbaya together, somehow the words will come true and all will be well in the world. But as soothing as the song may have sounded to me way back in 1971, when I hear those words now, in light of God's Word and what I now know of the spiritual warfare that's going on in the world today, it sounds to me like John Lennon, whether he realized it or not, was saying for us all to imagine that what God has told us is a lie. It sounds all too familiar, and reminiscent of the smooth-talking serpent in the Garden of Eden. As for me, I prefer to imagine all the things that God has promised us that are far better and have their foundation in scripture, **in truth**, rather than from the imaginations of a lost soul. At times I find myself trying to picture or imagine all the *details* of what God has in store for those who love Him, but I have a pretty clear picture of some of the things that I will find, because God has told us some of the things that we can expect when we arrive: We will see Jesus face-to-face; there will be no sorrow, no death, no pain, no tears, no regrets. The streets are paved in gold and the pure light of God illuminates all space. It will be a paradise type of environment, opulent in its beauty, jewels and gems abounding, beyond anything we've ever seen. I personally love sparkles and I picture everything to be sparkling all over the place! I've seen some spectacular places right here in this world, yet we're told that this world only hints at the beauty of God's eternal kingdom. There will be unspeakable joy flowing like rivers throughout the kingdom that God is preparing for us. Our bodies and our spirits will be rejuvenated completely, and we will not age or die.

"No eye has seen, no ear has heard, no mind can imagine the things that God has prepared for those who love Him" (1 Corinthians 13:12). "He will wipe away every tear from their eyes, and death shall be no more, neither shall there be mourning, nor crying, nor pain anymore, for the old things have passed away" (Revelation 21:4). "He will swallow up death forever. And the Lord God will wipe away the tears from every face" (Isaiah 25:18). "Your sun will no longer set and the moon will not wane; for the LORD will be your everlasting light, and the days of your sorrow will be over" (Isaiah 60:20). "Violence shall be no longer, neither waste or destruction within the borders; But you shall call your walls <u>Salvation</u>, and your gates will be called <u>Praise</u>" (Isaiah 60:18).

Of everything we have to look forward to, my favorite thought is this: Jesus will be right there with us, giving us comfort. "Fear not, for I have redeemed you; I have called you by your name" (Isaiah 43: 1). Imagine *that!*—He has called us by name! You had me at no sorrow, no death. Yes, it's going to be a whole new world! And although I'm still here for a time, I understand that this world isn't my real home. This life is just a testing ground of sorts and—when you consider eternity—a *very brief* journey toward my final destination. I'm continuously reminded of that truth every time another loved one dies. I don't want to be "so heavenly minded that I'm no earthly good." But on the other hand, I prefer that to being "So earthly minded that I'm no heavenly good." And I admit it's difficult. I want others to be aware of what God has in store for those who love Him. No one is promised tomorrow on this earth, but we have the promise of eternity in a place called heaven should we die tomorrow. I especially want my children and my friends and all those who haven't yet heard the gospel of salvation to be aware of what God is offering. I'm praying too that Christians around the world will wake up, start to get excited as prophecy continues to unfold, that they will draw closer to Him and truly consider what He has in store for them as they compare it to what the world has to offer. Meanwhile, just for fun, I wrote my own lyrics, inspired by the promises of God, that we can all sing with joy and confidence:

**"Imagine Heaven"**

Imagine there's a Kingdom
Where heaven will unfold
Shining with *pure* beauty
We'll walk on streets of gold.
Imagine all the people—dancing in the streets! You, yes, you too . . .

**You may say I'm a dreamer, but I know that this is true.**
**I hope someday you'll join me. There's a place prepared for you.**
Imagine there's no darkness,
Just God's eternal light.
No more sin or sadness
An endless future shining bright.
Imagine all the people living life in peace! You, yes, you too . . .
**You may say I'm a dreamer, but I know that this is true.**
**I hope someday you'll join me. I'll be waiting there for you.**
Imagine your new body,
It will never age or die.
Full of strength and glory
And we'll have eyes that never cry.
Imagine all the people, who will never shed a tear! You, yes, you too...
**You may say that I'm a dreamer, but I know that this is true.**
**I hope someday you'll join me. You'll learn of things you**
**never knew.**
Imagine death defeated,
No more pain and strife.
Nothing but joy and gladness,
Filling our eternal life.
Imagine all the people—singing songs of joy! You, yes, you too . . .
**You may say I'm a dreamer, but I know that this is true.**
**I hope someday you'll join me. And Jesus will be there too.**
Imagine you'll see Jesus,
You'll see Him face-to-face.
Imagine your emotion,
As you breathe in His loving grace.
Imagine all the people—Shouting cheers of praise! You, yes you
and me too . . .
**You may say I'm a dreamer, but I know that this is true.**
**I hope someday you'll join me. Everything will be brand new.**

"As for God, His ways are perfect. His word is flawless, He shields all who take refuge in Him."

## Chapter Eighteen

## JUSTICE AND GRACE

Now, I'm not God and I don't make the rules, but I can understand His dilemma. More than that, I truly appreciate His solution to the problem. The magnificence of God is revealed in all of this. This is undoubtedly a plan that only God could have come up with. His standard of *perfection, holiness, and justice* are only matched by His *grace, mercy, and love.* God took it upon Himself to satisfy the debt **we** owed. Wow—again a lot to wrap my head around, but that's what this means: "The wages of sin is death but the free gift of God is eternal life in Jesus Christ" (Romans 3:23). "He Himself bore our sins in His body . . . by

His wounds you have been healed" (1 Peter 2:24). I've heard people ask, "Why can't God simply wipe our slate clean? Why is a punishment or a sacrifice required?" First thing that comes to my mind is this: Who am I to question God? Surely He knows what He's doing and has a good reason for doing it. And the second thing is this: Regardless of why God requires a punishment or sacrifice, *He* took the punishment, made the sacrifice, and paid the debt Himself! Another thing that comes to mind is this: God told Adam right from the start what would happen if he and Eve chose to eat from the forbidden tree. God's laws don't change just because someone breaks them. According to God's perfect justice, the law still needed to be satisfied. And He took it upon Himself to do just that.

Although I can't emphatically answer the question of why God requires a blood sacrifice, however, I do know this: "God's ways are higher than our ways and His thoughts are higher" (Isaiah 55:9). We need to consider who God is. "Ascribe to the greatness of our God. He is the rock, His work is perfect for all *His ways are justice, a God of truth* and *without injustice*; Righteous and upright is He" (Deuteronomy 32:3). The Psalmist put it like this: "As for God, His ways are *perfect*. His word is flawless, He shields all who take refuge in Him" (Psalm 18:30). The more I began to understand the character of God as He has revealed Himself through the scriptures, I've come to the conclusion that *justice matters to God*. We should appreciate that! Most people I know feel very strongly, even passionately, about the concept of justice. We tend to be very much in favor of justice, especially when it comes to ourselves or someone we love. I know I do. We feel deeply about justice when **we** or a loved one are the victim of an injustice. So it shouldn't surprise anyone that the God and Creator of the universe requires justice. God had to set things right because of His own laws and His own nature of **righteousness**, perfection, holiness, justice, and so on. Every sin of mankind is a sin against God. *We* are the offenders. Yet God wrapped His justice in mercy by satisfying His absolute requirement of justice, Himself. The death sentence that belongs to us (the offenders) was paid for by Him. God's plan goes far beyond justice; it's incomprehensible, unimaginable, and may even sound convoluted, and yet that's exactly the way it is. "He Himself bore *our sins* in *His own body*" (1 Peter 2:24). *That's the Amazing Grace of God.*

"For God did not send His Son into the world to condemn the world but that the world through Him might be saved. Whoever believes in Him is not condemned. But those who do not believe are condemned already because they have not believed in the Only Son of God."
(1 John 3:17-18)

## *Chapter Nineteen*

## WHAT ARE WE BEING SAVED *FROM* ANYWAY?

I've spent a lot of time talking about life, death, sin, grace, faith, truth, God's love, and His gift of salvation. By now you may be asking yourself, *What are we being saved from anyway?* I don't want to spend too much time on the subject of hell, so I'll make this fire-and-brimstone portion brief. However, I would be remiss **not** to tell you just what it is that we're being saved from. Okay, here we go . . . According to the scriptures, we are being saved from going to a place where we will be "shut out from the presence of God" (2 Thessalonians 1:7–9). That thought alone scares the hell out of me. Yet that is one of the *mildest* descriptions of the place referred to as hell. It is also called a place of "everlasting

74

destruction" (Revelation 20:15) It's also described as "the fiery lake of burning sulfur, the blazing furnace, where there will be weeping and gnashing of teeth, the realm of the dead, a place where the fire never goes out" (Revelation 21:8, Matthew 13:42, Matthew 13:50, Acts 2:27, Mark 9:47–48). These and many other verses discuss and describe the subject of hell and who it is reserved for. The Bible speaks of hell as a very real place, and I believe it is, just as heaven is. But regardless of whether you take these verses literally or figuratively, it doesn't sound like a place where I or anyone I know or love would want to go and spend any amount of time, let alone our eternity .

I've found that most people are okay hearing about the **love** of God, but they become resentful and uncomfortable hearing about the wrath of God. However, both subjects are found in the scriptures. Although *many do*, I couldn't simply accept one and dismiss the other. Yes, we're told that there's "hell to pay" for those who choose **not** to believe in God and accept His gracious offer of salvation. Because of God's mercy, "It is *God's will* that NONE should perish," and God is long-suffering (2 Peter 3:9). It is *His desire* that everyone come to the saving knowledge of His grace. God's arm is reaching out to save us; however, God won't twist our arm or force His will on anyone. Nor will God's mercy compromise His perfect *judgment*, what He refers to as *His wrath*, to those who willfully choose **not** to come to Him for salvation. As from the beginning of time and creation, God has allowed us free will, and just as in life, our free will comes with consequences, both good and bad.

In this case, God's given each of us a choice, using our own free will to determine the outcome of our own eternity. Which is pretty awesome when you think about it. Throughout the scriptures again and again the choice is clear and nonnegotiable: "He who believes in the Son has everlasting life; and he who does not believe in the Son shall not see life, but the *wrath of God abides on him*" (John 3:36). People often use this following verse to convince themselves or others that they don't have to worry about God's condemnation: "For God did not send His Son into the world to condemn the world but that the world through Him might be saved." Conveniently they leave out the verse that comes directly after, which states: "Whoever believes in Him is not condemned. But whoever does not believe *stands condemned already* because they have not believed in the name of God's one and only Son" (1 John 3: 17-18). In other words, without the grace of God, we all have God's wrath looming over us. Many people struggle with or simply **reject** the idea that a loving God would send people to hell. But you can see by all of this that God does **not** want anyone to go to hell and it is "*His will* that none should perish," and so by that same token God does not send people to hell. It's our own free will to believe Him or not; that will direct the course for our own eternity. The concept of free will and consequence is nothing new to anyone; it's been around for centuries, and we all understand that simple concept. Jesus tells us very clearly and very specifically both the reward and the punishment of each scenario, and everyone must make the choice for themselves.

"Above all, you must understand that in the **last days** scoffers will come, scoffing and following their own evil desires. They will say, 'Where is this coming He promised?'..." (2 Peter 3:3-4)

## *Chapter Twenty*

## BACK WITH A VENGEANCE

Because of God's mercy, He will always give a warning to the nations, just as he did in the days of Noah. Noah was the only man who God found to be righteous during his time in a well-populated world that was full of wickedness and evil of every kind. Noah gave warnings of God's wrath to come to the people of his day for many years as he continued to build the ark as instructed by God. They all mocked him and laughed at him, and they went about their business as usual till the rains came, and the doors of the ark were shut before them, and they were utterly destroyed because of their disbelief. Noah warned them again and again. It was a swift judgment; however, it was preceded by a warning that lasted 120 years. The same was in the case of Sodom and Gomorrah, a lavish and opulent city full of every kind of immorality and depravity imaginable. So much that there were not even ten people within it to be found righteous. First came the warning to repent and turn to God, then came God's swift judgment. Lot was the only man found to be righteous. He and his family were spared from the destruction of the city. Although his wife did not take heed to the final warning: get out and *do not look back*. Therefore she wasn't spared even after she safely fled the city with her daughters and Lot, because she couldn't resist looking back at all the worldly riches she had left behind.

Through His word and through His people, God has been warning the nations for nearly two thousand years that His judgment is coming again to this world. He will be coming again to judge the nations for their unbelief and their utter rejection of Him, which have been made manifest in every kind of ungodliness and evil in the world today. People are quick to say, and I've heard it plenty: "A loving God would never do such a thing." They may very well be referring to the God of their own understanding, a God who they've custom-designed for themselves. However, they *cannot* make that statement about the God of the Bible, the God who is offering us all eternal life through His Son, Jesus.

God is a Loving God. Yes. He doesn't want anyone to die: "For I take no pleasure in the death of anyone, declares the Sovereign LORD. Repent and live" (Ezekiel 18:23). The word *repent* comes from the Greek word, metanoia; and regarding sin, simply means to change your mind, to turn around, make an about-face from it. That's God's desire, that we *repent and live*. But God has revealed Himself throughout the scriptures—both in the Old and New Testaments, among many descriptions—as a sovereign God, a holy God, a righteous God: "I form light and create darkness, I make peace and create calamity; I am the LORD, who does all these things. Shower, O heavens, from above, and let the skies pour down righteousness; let the earth open, that salvation and righteousness may bear fruit; let the earth cause them both to sprout; I the LORD have created it. *Woe to him who strives with his maker*, a pot among earthen pots! Does the clay say to him who forms it, 'What are you making?' Or shall your handiwork say 'your work has no handles'?" (Isaiah 45:7-9). God is also a jealous God. "I am the Lord your God; who brought you out of the land of Egypt, out of the house of bondage. You shall have NO other god before me" (Deuteronomy 5:6-7). And if you take a look at the Book of Revelation, ultimately, He is described as a God of Justice who will return to earth a second time in judgment to punish the ultimate sin, the sin of disbelief. We're told that He has promised and even reserved His wrath and a full display of vengeance for all those who have refused and rejected His grace, those who have mocked Him, those who have scoffed at His many warnings, those who thought they were so smart or so self-sufficient, who **chose** not to believe in God or their own need for forgiveness, those who have a *form of godliness*, but molded the word of God to fit their own intellect and liberal philosophies, and those for whatever reason who have chosen to live without Him. Jesus gave these words to the scoffers of His day as he spoke to them in front of the temple shortly before He was apprehended and put to death: "You are from beneath; I am from above. You are from this world. I am not of this world. Therefore, I say to you that you will die in your sins; for **you** *did not believe that I am HE,* you will die in your sins" (John 8:23). The apostle Paul gives us insight into how God views "the wisdom of man," those who think they're too intelligent to believe in God, as He has revealed Himself to us through His word: "Do not be deceived, If anyone among you *seems too wise* in this age, let him become a fool that he may become wise. For the wisdom of this world *is foolishness* with God. For it is written, 'He catches the wise in their own craftiness' and again, 'The Lord knows the thoughts of the wise, and knows that they are *futile*" (1 Corinthians 3:18–20). We're told by the apostle Peter, "Above all, you must understand that in the **last days** scoffers will come, scoffing and following their own evil desires. They will say, 'Where is this coming He promised?' But they deliberately overlook the fact that long ago *by God's word* the heavens existed and the earth was formed out of water and by water, through which the world of that time *perished in the flood*. And *by the same word*, the heavens and the earth *are reserved for fire*, being kept for the day of *judgement and destruction* of the ungodly...But do not forget this one thing dear friends: With the Lord, a day is like a thousand years, and a thousand years are like a day. The Lord is not slow in keeping His promise as some may think. Instead, *He is patient* with you, *NOT wanting anyone to perish*, but for everyone to come to repentance" (2 Peter 3:3–9). God is also described as a promise keeper; He will do what He has foreordained and will by no means break His word.

God is love; all of His attributes—whether they be holiness, perfection, mercy, and compassion or whether they be judgment and wrath—are encompassed in His *love*. No one would accuse or consider a parent who disciplines his or her child to be hateful or unloving. Parents understand that whether they're taking their child to Disneyland or giving them a spanking, both are done because they love them. Parents often say when it comes to discipline, "This hurts me more than it hurts you," even as the child may be saying "I hate you" or "You're mean." The parent understands how much they love them and knows what must be done. Although the stakes are much higher dealing with the rebellion of mankind and matters of eternity, the same principle holds true with the love of God. All of God's judgments come from **love**. Who are we to define or limit the parameters of His love according to what we agree with? We only know of love through God. We can't even begin to see or understand the magnitude of God: His infinite power, His righteousness, His holiness, His omniscience, His goodness, His mercy, His omnipotence, His judgment, and so on. We may not understand or consider His judgments as love because of our **finite** perception and definition of love. However, an infinite God of such magnitude I surely trust. We are eternal beings, and if God says an eternal judgment is required, I trust that He knows best. I assume He knows something that I don't know and has a very good reason for it. But from my very finite, human perspective as a parent, I would imagine that God doesn't want a bunch of unruly, ungrateful, prideful, rebellious humans who want to run their own show living in His perfect Kingdom. I remember telling a couple of my own children when they got to the age that they didn't think they had to listen to me or follow the house rules, (the rules of my kingdom) "If you want to run your own show, you're going to have to take it on the road."

It is a loving God who sent His beloved Son, Jesus, to die for your sins. It is a loving God who wants to save you and transform you, and bring you into all the joys of eternal life. And it is this same loving God who will bring wrath on those who reject it. I realize that people don't like ultimatums. But this is one that can't be avoided. I could just offer you a flowery message of forgiveness and of love as you choose to define it—sugar and spice and everything nice. I could leave out all this uncomfortable stuff about consequences, sin, and hell—all this narrow-minded stuff about Jesus being the only way to heaven—and as I said, many will. However, there is no "fine print" in the Bible; both are there in plain sight: the **good news**, His message of grace and forgiveness, as well as the **bad news** of His wrath and vengeance for those who refuse it. Both mercy and judgment are bound in love. I want to be sure not to leave anything out, even at the risk of offense. The inspired word of God isn't like a Build-A-Bear or a Build-A-Burger, where you can pick and choose the items you like. It's a package deal; you can take it or leave it *all*. We know about the grace, mercy, and long suffering of God through the very same holy scriptures that reveal the fury, judgment, and wrath of God. I can't accept **only** the words that I happen to like or just cling to the promises that make **me** feel good.

"Trust in the Lord with all your heart, and lean not on your own understanding. In all your ways acknowledge Him and He will direct your path." (Proverbs 3:5-6)

## Chapter Twenty One

# KEEP YOUR EYE ON THE COMPASS

Jesus said "I am the resurrection and the life. Whoever *believes* in Me, though he may die, he shall live." (John 11:25) What we choose to believe is a choice, and each choice will bring about a specific outcome. Let's say you come to a sign: THE BRIDGE IS COLLAPSED. DO NOT CROSS. The sign also offers you AN ALTERNATE ROUTE. You now have the choice: You can choose to believe what the sign is telling you and take the alternate route. Or you can choose to ignore the sign on the road and go with your own assessments and attempt to cross the bridge in spite of the warning. If you choose *not* to believe the warning and instead *choose* to cross the bridge, and you end up at the bottom of a ditch or a river, certainly you wouldn't blame the guy who went to the trouble to hang the warning sign. After all, you were given another option and you made the choice *not* to believe it. If you have been offered ample reason to believe through reasonable, previously reliable information that it is going to be thirty degrees outside and raining (clouds lingering above, you can hear the wind howling, the local weather forecast tells you, etc.), it would likely result in you choosing to dress warmly, wear a raincoat, and bring an umbrella, thereby keeping you from being cold and getting wet and possibly sick. If you have been offered ample reason to believe that your car is low on fuel (the "low fuel" light is on, the fuel gauge is in the "red zone"), it would likely result in you heading to the nearest gas station, thereby saving yourself from being stranded somewhere down the road.

We all make choices to believe and act on hundreds if not thousands of things throughout our lives with very limited information. Sometimes it pans out, other times it doesn't. When it comes to whether or not to believe in **Jesus**, we have far more reason than a sign on the road; we have signs everywhere fulfilling the very words He spoke more than two thousand years ago. Because His word has not been wrong yet, I have **no** doubt that believing in Jesus will pan out for me, and for everyone who places their eternity in His hands. This brings me back to something my mom used to say when I was a little girl. She used to give us warnings all the time about various things, such as jumping off a chest of drawers onto my bed, for example. For our own safety, she would warn us of the danger in doing that. And I remember she would often add these final words to her instruction and warning: "... Don't come crying to me." In other words, she gave me fair warning *because she loved me*. If I chose **not** to believe her and listen to her instruction, and I ended up getting hurt doing the very thing that she had told us **not** to do, I had only myself to blame. Believing in God's offer of salvation *through faith in Jesus* is **a** choice, and we have been given *ample reason* to believe in Him.

We have been given more than *ample reason* to believe in the divine nature of **Jesus** through the firsthand recorded accounts given by His closest followers, who had nothing to gain and yet risked their very lives to share this message, these accounts that stand stronger under scrutiny in the face of historical scholars than any other written, recorded accounts of ancient history. I don't know anyone who doubts the *existence* of George Washington, Alexander The Great and others whose existence is known through the written historical records, yet I don't know anyone who's ever seen any of them. In the same way, we have solid evidence of the existence of Jesus: We have His detailed genealogy and firsthand accounts from those who knew Him personally. We have the supernatural events surrounding His birth, the miracles of His life and ministry, and His resurrection from death to life, all recorded in our history and passed down from generation to generation. The **existence** of Jesus as a historical figure is validated by other ancient writings and historical accounts outside of the biblical writings. So considering the evidence we have, it stands to reason that the same will be true when we choose to believe in Jesus and His offer of salvation. From that moment on, the Spirit of God lives within the believer. His role according to the scripture is to be their helper, their advocate, their comforter; He is with us **all the time** to help us in every decision we come to. As we yield to the Spirit of God, we can hardly help but make good choices. However, in spite of the Holy Spirit's indwelling, we still have our *free will*. The Holy Spirit does **not** strong-arm His hosts. Rather He gently guides them and shows them the right paths. Distractions or temptations of life may come along, and just as we may not pay attention to or ignore the weather forecast or the fuel gauge, that choice will result in unnecessary trouble in our lives each time we choose to disregard the leading of our God, the Good Shepherd. But we are learning as we go, and God is with us every step of the way, even when we fall. "He will **never** leave us nor forsake us" (Deuteronomy 31:8, Joshua 1:5, Hebrews 13:15), and we know "*Nothing* can separate us from the love that is in Christ Jesus" (Romans 8:35). I often use this analogy when talking about the Spirit of God; I liken the Spirit of God to a "moral compass." Christians have the Spirit of God living within them from the moment they truly believe and place their faith in Jesus. However, many times we lean on our own understanding, we get busy or distracted, and we don't pay attention to the Spirit of God. That's when we get into trouble, lose our way and find ourselves at the bottom of a spiritual ditch, and I speak from experience. In the same way, if we travel with a compass, but never take it out of our pocket, our compass will be of **no help**, and we're likely to end up floundering and lost. But if we continue to set our eyes on the compass and follow its leading, we'll stay on the right path until we reach our destination, which is heaven. "In all your ways acknowledge Him and He will direct your path" (Proverbs 3:6).

"For you formed my innermost being;
You knit me together in my mother's womb." (Psalm 139:13)

# *Chapter Twenty Two*

## JESUS LOVES THE LITTLE CHILDREN (AND EVERYONE ELSE TOO)

People often ask this question: "What about the people in remote parts of the world who may not have the opportunity to hear about Jesus, and what about children, babies, and what about the mentally impaired who don't have the capacity to hear or understand?" Although many times that question is asked as a diversion, or for the sake of argument, with no sincere desire for an answer; it is a legitimate question, so I'll try my best to answer it here: Jesus shed His blood for all mankind for the forgiveness of sins. His sacrifice was paid "once for all," past, present, and future sins. Remember, the Old Testament prophets never knew about Jesus specifically as we now do, since He hadn't been born yet. Still, they were saved and were covered by the blood of Jesus, which hadn't **yet** been shed, simply because they had faith in God and His divine promise and plan for mankind. We're told that "Abraham *believed* the Lord and his *faith* was counted unto him *as righteousness*" (Genesis 15:6, Romans 4:3).

This is God's promise: "If you seek Me, you will find Me, if you search for me with all of your heart" (Jeremiah 29:13, Deuteronomy 4:29, Proverbs 8:17, Matthew 7:7). God sees into the hearts and hears the prayers of every single person no matter where in the world they are. No one seeking God and *desiring* **truth** will be overlooked. The apostle Paul says that "God is a rewarder of those who earnestly seek Him" (Hebrews 11:6). Anyone seeking God today can't help but to find Jesus, the way, *the truth*, and the life. And it's up to each individual how they will respond once they find it. God is always true to His word. It seems to me that Christians are asked to take the gospel to the ends of the earth so that they can take part in God's plan of salvation; thereby they can also take part in the blessings and joy that come with it. If there are seeking hearts out there in remote places, no matter where they are, God will be sure to send someone carrying the good news of salvation to them. He knows *exactly* where they can be found. And there are thousands of testimonies from people who were found in the most unlikely and remote places and uncivilized tribes in the world, who have had the gospel delivered to them, bringing them to salvation. Although surely God, the Creator of all things, doesn't **need** our help to accomplish His will, I trust that He has a good reason in allowing us to take part in the gathering together of all those who will be with Him and with all believers for eternity.

When it comes to the question about children, babies, and those who are mentally incapable of hearing or understanding the gospel, I can't help but trust in the goodness, mercy and character of God. And I can also look to His word for an answer to that concern. I think of when the Israelites disobeyed God in the wilderness, God said that *they* would **not** be allowed to cross over to the Promised Land. But look what He said to them about the children: "As *for your little ones*, who you said would become a prey, and *your children*, who today have no knowledge of good or evil, *they shall enter*. And to them I will give it and they shall possess it" (Deuteronomy 1:39). There are many both Old and New Testament verses that illustrate the tenderness of God toward the children. Jesus said, "Let the little children come to me, and do not hinder them, for the Kingdom of heaven belongs to such as these" (Matthew 18:3, Matthew 19:24). Jesus had a tender heart for children, so much that he warned, "It would be better for a man to have a millstone hung around his neck and thrown into the sea than for him to cause one of these little ones to stumble" (Luke 17:2, Matthew 8:6). Yes, Jesus loves the little children, *all* the children of the world. They were precious to Him even before they were born. "For you formed my innermost being; You knit me together in my mother's womb." (Psalm 139:13) We can trust in God and rest assured that no baby, child, or person without the ability to comprehend good and evil will be left behind, because they are precious to Him. God is not only *just and fair*; He is *merciful and abounding in loving kindness*.

"If you seek me you will find me when you seek with all of your heart."
(Jeremiah 29:13)

## *Chapter Twenty-Three*

## WITHOUT EXCUSE

Let's be honest: the truth of the matter is that the gospel of God's grace through faith in Jesus is being spread throughout the world today like no other time in history. You may even have heard about Jesus since you were a child; I don't know anyone who hasn't at least heard of Jesus, and most have even heard that He died on the cross for our sins. Bibles are abundantly available to nearly everyone. It seems obvious to me that the problem is a "heart problem" rather than a "lack of ability to hear the message problem." After all, think about this: you, right now, are hearing the good news, and yet you may still be wavering and looking for reasons to reject the offer. Many others have done the same, and many more will do the same when their opportunity arises. The fact is that people will continue to come up with all kinds of reasons not to believe in or accept Jesus's offer of salvation. And I continue to pray for them all. God knows the heart of every person. He not only knows that there will be millions of people who **will hear** and yet **will reject** His gracious offer; God also knows exactly who they are. And although their rejection grieves Him deeply, this process of sifting the chaff from the wheat and separating the goats from the sheep will continue and is being fulfilled for the eternal purposes of God for the sake of His Eternal Kingdom.

For those of us who have heard and *do* have the ability to understand, I ask that you consider the very nature of God as He has revealed Himself: a God of justice who is unchanging; merciful; long-suffering; full of truth, mercy, and grace—a God who loves us so much that He sent His only begotten Son to pay the price for our sins. This God revealed to us, is a *personal* God, He's *not* some impersonal cosmic force. He knows us personally, and He loves each and every one of us *personally*. We can trust that God will never go against His own nature.

God has chosen His most prized creation on earth, *mankind*, to reveal Himself to us all. Through His chosen prophets, we have the scriptures. *That was no accident*. The Bible is a compilation of sixty-six literary books encompassing history, poetry, and prophecy, penned by more than forty authors over the course of thousands of years, and yet the more you study it, the more you can see one continuous theme, each book fitting perfectly together as if written by *one* author. From beginning to end it carries the same theme of God's love, judgment and redemption throughout. It is *God's prophetic blueprint*, recording not only events of the **history** of mankind. He's given His instructions for us to live our **present** life to the fullest as well as recording the prophecies foretelling the *future* of the human race and the planet. God has covered it *all*—past, present, and future. The Bible stands apart from all other ancient religious writings, and apparently its content is so impressive that major religions from the Buddhists to the Muslims have added portions to their own religious writings. Other more modern-day religious cult founders who claim to be Christians, such as Joseph Smith, Mary Baker Eddy, Charles Taze Russel and others, place the Bible alongside their own written doctrine, perhaps to add credibility. However, they've made subtle but significant changes to it, in order to line up with their particular, deceptive message, giving Jesus a demotion, referring to Him as a prophet or teacher, each denying Jesus as the Eternal Son of God and the Savior of the world. Satan is the author of every false religion, and remember it's his primary mission to keep people in the darkness so they won't come to the light. So far he's doing a great job!

Through mankind, using His chosen people, God brought His inspired written word to us, and through mankind He brought the living word, His only begotten Son, **Jesus**, into the world to reveal Himself: The apostle John tells us: "In the beginning was the word, the word was *with* God and the word *was* God . . . and *the word became flesh* and dwelt among us" (John 1:1, John 1:14). Jesus said, "If you have seen me, you've seen the Father." "I and the Father are One" (John 14:9). Jesus also tells us, "If you are *of the truth*, you would know me." God has also chosen His own creation of the world to reveal Himself to us, revealing Himself through nature and creation, and He's revealed Himself through our moral conscience as well. This is the way the apostle Paul explains it: "For since the creation of the world, God's invisible qualities, the eternal power and divine nature have been clearly seen, being understood from what has been made, so that men are *without excuse*" (Romans 1:20). He tells us that the knowledge of God is written on our hearts. Paul is telling us that according to God, whether men deny His existence or not; *everyone* has an inherent knowledge of God through His creation, and that everyone has a built-in, God-given conscience, and *everyone* will be accountable for the *knowledge* they have been given when they stand before God.

You may have heard of "Pascal's wager." Blaise Pascal was a seventeenth-century French philosopher, theologian, mathematician, a physicist and a Christian, who came to the conclusion that if man were betting on the existence of God, we'd do well to wager that God exists, concluding that it's our "best bet." I never had the pleasure of meeting my husband's mom, as she passed away a few years before we met, but from all accounts, she was a very special woman. She survived two husbands, each of whom tragically died at a young age. She was beautiful, kind-hearted, and she was a very strong-spirited mom. She single-handedly raised two boys and two girls. My husband has often reminisced about something in particular that she used to say when he was a kid that stuck with him: "If you don't listen, you're going to have to feel." There is a lot of wisdom in those words. I believe putting your faith in Jesus is your best bet. "If you seek me you will find me when you seek with all of your heart" (Jeremiah 29:13). "But if from there you seek the LORD your God, you will find Him if you seek Him with all your heart and with all of your soul" (Deuteronomy 4:29).

"The God who made the world and everything in it is the Lord of heaven and earth and does not live in temples built by human hands. And He is not served by human hands, as if he needed anything. Rather, *He Himself gives everyone life and breath and everything else.* From one man He made all Nations, that they should inhabit the whole earth; and He *marked out their appointed times* in history and the boundaries of their lands. God did this *so that they would seek Him* and perhaps reach out for Him and *find Him,* though He is not far from any one of us. *For in Him we live, move, breathe and have our being.* As some of your own poets have said, 'We are His offspring.'" (Acts 17:24–28). So I say unto you: "Ask and it will be given to you; *seek and you will find*; knock and it will be opened to you" (Luke 11:9). "They show that the work of the law is written on their hearts. Their consciences confirm this. Their competing thoughts either *accuse or even excuse*" (Romans 2:15). So when we stand before God, we may stand there stammering on as we try to rationalize our rejection of Him, and His offer of salvation but we will be *without excuse.*

"Therefore I do not run like someone running aimlessly;
I do not fight like a boxer beating the air." (1 Corinthians 9:26)

# Chapter Twenty-Four

## THE BIG GAME

Another question people ask: "If God already **knows** what's going to happen, how can you say that we have free will?" *God is not bound by time.* Although the wonders and majesty of God are far beyond my understanding, I will do my best to answer this question in my very *limited* wisdom, using this scenario: Okay, so there's a big championship game on ESPN that I don't want to miss. This game is taking place at a very specific space in time, beginning at 6:00 on Saturday evening. I have a previous pressing commitment, so I won't be home to watch it. However, I set my TV to record it, and I have plans to watch it later when I get home. That championship game is scheduled during a very specific space in time, but because of today's technology, I am not bound within that specific space in time in order to watch it. However, while I'm on my way home to watch the big game for myself, a friend of mine calls me. He's very excited, and before I can say a word, he begins by telling me who won the game. Then he goes on to give me a blow-by-blow of the game—each and every play, every foul, every injury, and so on. So now by the time I get to watch the game for myself, I already know exactly what is going to happen. **Yet** I didn't cause any of it to happen. I didn't have anything to do with any of the decisions made that led to and determined the outcome of the game. Each player, coach, referee, and so on *had free will* to make the decisions they made throughout the game from the beginning to the end of that particular space in time.

We are here on this earth **now** during this very specific space in time and history. *We are bound within that time; God is not. He* already knows the past, the present, and the future. God is outside of time, He has already seen the game and all the highlights of history, so to speak, and *He knows how the game ends.* He knows the winners and the losers; He saw each play as it was called and watched as each was executed. However, *we* are still here, bound within this specific time period; we are still playing this game of life. While we are here, we are in it to win it, so to speak. "I have fought the good fight, I have finished the race, I have kept the faith. Now there is in store for me the crown of righteousness, which the Lord, the righteous Judge, will award to me on that day—and not only to me, but also to *all who have longed for His appearing*" (2 Timothy 4:7–9). And not only is Jesus cheering us on and anxiously waiting for us at the championship banquet; He has offered us His own Holy Spirit to help us along the way, with each and every stride as we focus on the prize, until we cross the finish line. "Therefore I do not run like someone running aimlessly; I do not fight like a boxer beating the air" (1 Corinthians 9:2)

"Today is the day of salvation." (2 Corinthians 6:2, Hebrews 3:15)

## *Chapter Twenty-Five*

# WHAT! NOT EVERYONE'S GOING TO HEAVEN?

I understand how difficult it is as we consider all of these things. We've all heard or offered words of comfort, such as these when someone dies: "They're in a better place now." "They're finally at peace." "They're not suffering anymore." "We'll see them again in heaven." As comforting as those words may *sound*, that may not be the truth for everyone who has died. According to what we know from the scriptures, millions upon millions of people from all generations past and present, will **not** be going to heaven. They will be separated from God; they will greatly suffer throughout eternity because of their disbelief and *willful rejection* of God's salvation for them. That's a difficult pill for anyone to swallow and that truth may keep many from wanting to except Jesus as their Savior. I want to offer hope to those and to everyone who has lost a loved one. As a believer who will be spending my eternity in heaven with God, and who has lost *many* loved ones, it was tough for me to accept too. As unpopular as that may sound, as hard as it is to accept this reality, I realize the word of God is clear on this issue. Everyone is familiar with the common expression, "The truth hurts." At the same time, we understand that ultimately, often times the truth is the very thing we *need* to hear and accept. Many times *the truth* is excruciatingly painful to come to terms with, but it doesn't change the facts of the truth.

One of those times comes to my mind; although it's so personal and still very painful to recall, I felt it may be helpful here. A few years ago, I heard the most excruciating and painful words that I could have ever imagined hearing: A little over three years ago, in the very early hours of the morning, it was barely light out when I heard my husband's cell phone ring from across the bed. Still half asleep as I listened, I could faintly hear the voice of my son, Jimmy, telling my husband that my daughter, Nichol was dead! She was struck by a drunk driver and killed instantly, as she stood on the side of the road, at 4:00 on the evening before. My son called my husband so that he could break the devastating news to me personally. But in the quietness of the early morning, I heard my son's voice through the phone saying those heart-wrenching words, "Nichol is dead." I instantly broke into a million pieces emotionally. I was in denial, fighting against the truth of those words: insisting there had to be some mistake. Then as they set in, I was completely inconsolable for a time that morning. And for the days that followed, I was a mess. People began coming and going from the house. I did my best to be polite and hold my composure, but I just wanted to sleep. I thought that if I could sleep long enough, I would wake up, and *the truth* of her death would be gone; it wouldn't be true anymore and I would find that it was just a bad dream. But there it was–each time I woke, the truth was still there: my daughter is dead, and it was final. My heart was shattered and through the grace of God, is still on the mend today. I simply didn't want to believe it was true. But nothing I did, could change that truth.

We all have loved ones who have died ahead of us, and we wonder about them. "Will they be there when I arrive?" We all know of many wonderful, really nice, much-loved people who have spent their entire lives doing many self-sacrificing, benevolent, kind-hearted things. They heard the gospel at some time during their lives, but (as far as anyone knew) they never made the decision to accept Jesus as their Savior. They may even have said that they "believe in God" but that "Jesus, forgiveness, and Bible stuff" just wasn't for them. Instead they went through their entire lives with faith that their own goodness was enough, doing what they thought was right in their own eyes, they hoped for the best. We may wonder, "What about them? They were so sweet, so kind, so generous and selfless. Will they be accepted into heaven?"

We know that according to scripture, they will not meet God's requirement if they have based their assurance of getting into heaven in what they consider their own goodness instead of placing their faith in the sacrifice of His Son, Jesus. We can't know the innermost thoughts and hearts of many seemingly wonderful people based on our limited knowledge. But God's knowledge is infinite. God knows their hearts; He's seen straight through to their every thought and their every motive in every decision throughout their entire life, He knows of every time His offer of salvation and eternal life was extended to them. We also know that God is merciful and just; He gives each of us *every opportunity* to come to Him right up to our last breath.

Using the opportunities that God has presented, I've shared the gospel over the course of many years with many people. For the most part, after hearing the message of God's grace, they opted out for whatever reason by the choice of their own free will. And it is certainly their prerogative to do so. It's not my job to save anyone, but to plant a seed of **truth** when I can, and pray that it grows; pray that maybe somewhere down the road, someone else will water the sprout of truth and it will pop up and continue to grow into faith. Because we're told, "without faith, it is impossible to please God" (Hebrews 11:6). Not faith in just anything, but faith in the TRUTH. As I said before, everyone has faith in something. But it is the object of your faith that will be considered when God looks into our hearts. When I share with people and the message is rejected or casually dismissed, all I can do is pray for God to continue to work in their hearts, **and I do**. One thing is for sure: "You can lead a horse to water, but you can't make them drink." As disheartened as I may become at times, I continue to pray that they will one day drink from the living waters of God's grace. I hope to see all of my loved ones who have died ahead of me when I arrive, but I don't know their hearts like God does. I have many family members and friends who I've been praying for, for years, and many of those I've lost over the years. For those loved ones I *wonder* about, I've found comfort during my times of loss and deep grieving as I remember the story of the thief on the cross who hung next to Jesus. The thief recognized *in his last moment* of life that *Jesus was his only hope*, and he cried out to Him as he was dying: "Jesus, remember me when you come into your Kingdom" (Luke 23:42–43). Jesus, even as He was dying Himself, comforted the thief next to Him and assured him of his salvation; as the thief took his last breath, Jesus let him know that He would be with him in paradise. Keep in mind, that thief was a guilty man, he had spent a lifetime being a thief and possibly worse, yet he was saved because of his faith in Jesus, in the very last moment of his life. That brings hope to all of us who have lost loved ones.

As for my precious daughter, Nichol; during my darkest time of grieving her loss, I was blessed beyond measure and comforted by God: I knew that as a little girl, she had accepted Jesus as her Savior, she had memorized many bible verses at her Children's Church group and so on. I clung to that with both fists, because as an adult she had wondered off the path and was struggling with many things as well as with various addictions. I prayed that the seed of faith that was planted when she was a child had taken root and not been plucked away. (Matthew 13:1-23) But God in His mercy gave me a gift, in fact He gave me two gifts during that time shortly after her death: Among her property that was collected and retrieved by the Highway Patrol at the crash-site, was her purse. Inside it was a book that she had been reading, with a little paper marker in it where she left off. She loved to read, and like my friend, she was always in the middle of one book or another and sometimes she'd even have two going at once. The book in her purse was called "Grace, Healing and Hope," the little marker she had placed inside where she left off was between two chapters, one on each side: The chapter on the left was – "Judgement Day Honesty" and the chapter on the right – "Settle The Matter." My heart leapt as I saw that. I read the book myself since, finding that it beautifully articulated the pure gospel of Jesus and I was greatly blessed by it, as I'm sure she was. I believe that God gave me that gift with her property as further *assurance* and comfort that I would see her again. The other gift came shortly after, by way of her teenage daughter, Angel, who was staying with me and my husband at the time of her Mom's death, and for the two and a half years after as well: A couple weeks before Nichol died, Angel had spent a night with her Mom. That was the last time she saw her. After Nichol's death, Angel told me about their last time together and particularly about something that happened while she and her mom were in the car together, on their way back to my house early the next morning. She said as they were driving along the highway, for some reason the car radically swerved, scaring the heck out of them, causing them both a momentary panic. As soon as they both got their bearings back, Nichol said these very words to Angel: "I'm not afraid to die because **I know** I'm going to Heaven **because** Jesus died for my sins." Again, my heart leapt at the sound of those words. Oh, the tender mercies of God, to so graciously give these perfect gifts to me!

Anyway, God knows the hearts of every person, and He is waiting to hear from them, waiting for them to cry out to Him, *even in the last moment or breath of their lives.* We can continue to hold out hope for the many of those who we may be unsure of. They, like the thief on the cross, may have cried out to Jesus in their last breath. Maybe they recalled someone telling them about Jesus being the *only* way to His Father in heaven, "the **W**ay the **T**ruth and the **L**ife." They may have cried out to Jesus in that moment. Maybe they heard a message about the saving grace of Jesus from a friend or even a stranger that stuck with them—it didn't sink in at the time, but in their last breath, they believed and they called out to Him. Maybe they even accepted Jesus as their Savior at some point, and they believed in their heart but had wandered off the path, or maybe they put their faith in Jesus, but didn't openly share because they were worried that they would face an onslaught of ridicule or persecution. All of these things and many more are possible. God is full of mercy and He's *all ears* when it comes to the prayers of those who call on Him for forgiveness and salvation.

The bottom line is this: God will not force anyone to believe and accept His offer, but He continues to give *everyone* the opportunity right up to their last breath. Regardless of anything, whether or not you are blessed with a special gift of comfort as I was, there is a deep comfort in *knowing the sovereignty of God* and His immeasurable mercy: God wants *everyone* to come to Him and be saved. There is no doubt that everyone who seeks God, will hear the gospel of Jesus Christ. No one will slip through the cracks when it comes to His salvation. God won't be saying "Oh darn, I missed that one, or sorry, I stepped away for a minute and I didn't hear you." His word tells us that He *rewards* those who earnestly seek Him. The reward is that they will find *the truth* and their own salvation into eternal life. It is *God's perfect sovereignty* that brings me assurance and comfort. Because of that I understand that if anyone I'm hoping to see in heaven isn't there when I arrive, although it will break my heart; I'll know it *wasn't* God's choice, but rather it was *their own choice* that kept them from coming. When I was a little girl, I remember that my dad always kept a "hanky" in his pocket; he kept it handy, always ready to wipe away tears and all kinds of other things. I like to think that our heavenly Father has one too, and He has it ready for His children for that very time. "And God shall wipe away all tears from their eyes; and there shall be no more death, neither sorrow, nor crying, neither shall there be any more pain: for the former things are passed away ... And the one sitting on the throne said 'Behold, I make all things new.'" (Revelation 21: 4)

There is so much **we** don't know, but there is **nothing** that God doesn't know. If you are reading this, then you're still alive, which means that it's *not too late* to call on Jesus: whether you've been sitting on the fence or even if you've openly rejected Him your entire life, and no matter what you've done or where in your life you are, He's waiting to hear from you, He's waiting for you to call on Him. "Everyone who calls upon the name of the Lord will be saved." (Romans 10:13 Acts 2:21) Don't miss your opportunity. Call on Jesus; He truly **is** the *only* way, just as He has said. You can trust and find comfort in the sovereignty of God, and don't let your worries about your loved ones who have died before you, keep you from accepting what God is offering you **today** while you still have breath, because there is no promise of tomorrow. "Today if you hear His voice, do not harden your heart..." (Hebrews 3:15).

"And He will judge the world in righteousness;
He will execute judgement with equity." (Psalm 8:9)

## Chapter Twenty-Six

## GOD'S CALLING THE SHOTS

I trust in the mercies of God even as I realize that His mercy will **in no way** alleviate His perfect judgment, which is impending for those who have made a clear choice to go it on their own, without Jesus. As I mentioned earlier, the apostle, John, tells us the very reason that people reject God's offer: "This is the judgement, that the light has come into the world, and men loved darkness rather than the light; for their deeds were evil" (John 3:19). Notice John didn't say, "This might be a possibility." He said, "This is the judgement." The apostle Paul says it like this: "They will perish because they *refused* to come to *the truth* and so be saved" (2 Thessalonians 2:10). It's the natural instinct of mankind to want everything our own way and to blame someone if we don't get it.

I was sitting in on a conversation between two dear friends of mine, after one of our regular Sunday dinners a few months back. They were discussing someone they knew who wanted some specific project done at his very upscale home. It was the home of a very wealthy and entitled celebrity whose name I won't mention, but as many celebrities, he's used to getting what he wants. The contractor he hired assessed the job that the wealthy homeowner wanted done and he strongly advised against it, explaining that there may be safety issues or future structural problems. But the owner insisted he still wanted it done, in spite of the contractor's advice. The contractor reluctantly agreed to do the work for the spoiled celebrity, but to protect himself from the liability of future problems, a clause was written into the contract noting that they advised against the particular project for the reasons of safety and structure. As it turned out, later down the road the very issues that the contractor warned of did become a problem. The wealthy homeowner was so upset that he sued the contractor! That's audacity! Naturally my two friends expressed their disgust at the homeowner, and I thoroughly agreed. The homeowner was warned it was a bad idea, but he made the choice to do it anyway, and he wanted someone to blame when the contractor's warning became a reality. (By the way, the wealthy celebrity, homeowner lost in court.) In the same way, God has warned us about the danger of not accepting Jesus as our Savior; He is giving us opportunity after opportunity to come to Him and has given many warnings about what will happen if we don't. So we can't blame (or sue) God if things don't work out the way we wanted, and we end up in hell. That too would be audacity! We may not like the conditions of God's plan, but whether we like it or not, He's calling the shots. After all, He is God.

It is *God's will* that *none* should perish, and as He said, He takes no pleasure in the death of anyone. That's why He has imparted to us *everything we need to know* to be saved. I trust in the judgments of God, because I know they're perfect. I know our God is a *sovereign* God, which means He is a *righteous* ruler. Unlike us, unlike the rulers and judges of this fallen world, God sees all and He knows all; there is no evidence suppressed that He hasn't seen. He has thoroughly and extensively reviewed each and every case, so we can rest assured knowing that whatever His judgments, *they will be fair, just, and perfect*, and when we see Him face-to-face, we will understand too. God does not arbitrarily or randomly send people to hell; hell is a choice everyone makes for themselves when they refuse His offer to save them. Like I said, you can't blame the guy who went to the trouble to hang the warning sign... Remember, God's arm is reaching out to save you, but God will in no way twist anyone's arm — He's not interested in dragging people through the gates of heaven kicking and screaming. God is pleading with mankind to accept His offer of salvation, which is only through His precious Son, Jesus. It's our choice to take heed of His calling or ignore it. In the end, everyone will get what they choose. "Today if you hear His voice, do not harden your heart..." (Hebrews 3:15).

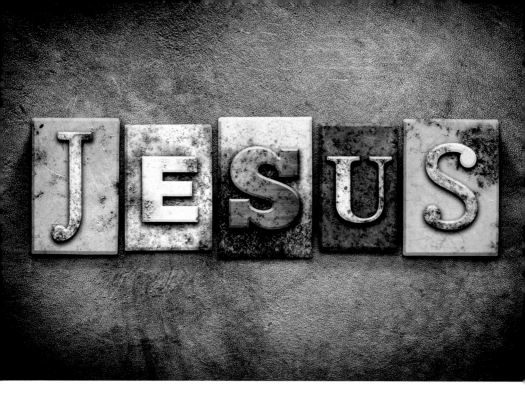

"Salvation exists in **no one else**, for there is **no other name** given under heaven by which we *must* be saved." (Acts 4:12)

## *Chapter Twenty-Seven*

### "JUST BECAUSE YOUR FRIENDS DO SOMETHING STUPID . . ."

God is the King of His own Kingdom. Without a special key, so to speak, the Kingdom is impenetrable. *Jesus* is the key, the only key that will open the gate to the Kingdom of Heaven. He's given warnings to those who may attempt to enter their own way, without the special key; He is urging you to come to Him and enter into His loving fortress and spend eternity with Him. He has made it abundantly clear that *no amount of good works will be of any help to you if you show up at the gate without that all-important key.* The gate simply cannot be opened without it. As I mentioned earlier, it's like showing up, right on time for the job interview, all dressed up and fully prepared with an amazing résumé, but you don't have the *necessary* passcode to get into the building; your amazing résumé will be *worthless* to you. God is offering you *the key* to the kingdom even now: **JESUS**. He's giving you *the passcode* to the building: **JESUS**. "Salvation exists in *no one else*, for there is *no other name* given under heaven by which we must be saved" (Acts 4:12). Why wait until your last breath? Especially as you consider that you don't even know when or where your last breath will be taken.

Something I've often heard people say over the years when addressing the idea of going to hell, usually in a cavalier, dismissive manner: "Well, I don't care if I go to hell because all of my friends will be there." They laugh it off as if there will be a big party going on down there. Unfortunately it will be one *hell* of a party, and nobody will be having any fun. The reality of that breaks my heart. It reminds me of something else my Mom used to say, and yours may have too: "Just because your friends do something stupid doesn't mean you have to do it."

Of course *I want everyone to go to heaven.* I love my family and my friends so much. But I don't want to hang out with them, or anyone, in hell. Where's the fun in that? I know that misery loves company, but I've had my fill of misery. And believing as I do, I'm not willing or foolish enough to say, "That's not fair! If everyone can't go to heaven *on their own terms*, then I would rather go to hell and hang out with my friends who willingly turned down such a gracious offer." I urge you to give careful consideration to *the evidence and claims of Jesus* and to accept His offer of eternal life through faith in Him. "Behold I stand at the door and knock. If anyone should hear My voice and open the door, then I will come in to him and will dine with him and he with Me" (Revelation 3:20). "Behold, now is the time of God's favor; now is the day of salvation." (2 Corinthians 6:2)

"That which is born of flesh, is flesh, and that which is born of Spirit, is spirit. Do not marvel that I said to you, 'You must be born again.'"
(John 3:6-7)

## Chapter Twenty-Eight

## PLAN OF GOD OR PLAN OF MAN?

Contemplating the plans and religions of mankind, they all have something in common. *Man's plans* are conceived and set forth with the goal of exalting themselves. The plans of men spring with hope of power, praise, pride, and wealth; they're plans that are designed to give men the sense of accomplishment, success, or personal satisfaction and ultimately a sense of self-worth or pride, and a good pat on the back. The same goes with *man's religions*. All world religions (with the exception of Christianity) call for man's attempt to *work or earn* his way to God or godhood—such as knocking on doors, lighting candles, doing good deeds, meditating, offering sacrifices, donating to charitable causes, fulfilling sacraments, attending church, volunteering at a homeless shelter—all of which, in a matter of time turn into pride.

Christianity, on the other hand tells us plainly: "All have sinned and fallen short of the glory of God." (Romans 3:23). And it tells us further "The wages of sin is death, but the *gift of God* is eternal life through Jesus Christ our Lord." (Romans 6:23) Christianity says "For by grace you have been saved through faith, and that not of yourselves; it is the gift of God, not of works, lest anyone should boast" (Ephesians 2:8–9). *God's plan* reveals God reaching out to us, offering us His free, undeserved gift of salvation. Telling us that we are saved *by faith*, *not* by works! This is amazing and a foreign concept to mankind. There is certainly nothing wrong with doing good deeds, trying to be a good person, meditating, or volunteering at a homeless shelter. They're all admirable, and I highly encourage all of them. But Christians realize that *without Jesus*, there is *no amount of* "good deeds" that will get them into heaven; they realize and accept their own vulnerability, being born into sin. God's plan offers *forgiveness for the sins of mankind* by accepting the "once for all" sacrifice of Jesus's death on the cross on their behalf. No one except God is exalted in God's plan. As it should be. Of God's salvation, we're told, "It is a *gift* of God, not of works [so] that *no man can boast*." (Ephesians 2:9) Yikes, God just threw a monkey wrench into any plans we may have come up with on our own, because mankind loves to boast! "Look at me, see what I did, see what I've got, see how hard I work, see how nice I am, see how religious I am." On the other hand, God's plan offers this amazing gift of salvation—which leads to eternal life—but *requires* that mankind recognize and acknowledge that without God they would not have or be able to do anything, that their very existence is a gift from God. Most importantly, that they are in need of this gift of salvation, that they are utterly *helpless to save themselves*; beyond that, they need to realize that anything they do *apart from God*, no matter how good they may think it is, has any eternal or spiritual value. Isaiah the prophet said it like this: *Apart from God* "all *our own* righteousness is like filthy rags" (Isaiah 64:6). God's plan tells us that **only** the things done with **this** realization of ourselves and of God will carry us into eternity. On the other bright and shining side of the coin is this: Those who put their *faith in Jesus* are covered by His grace and are *counted as righteous* before a Holy God when they face eternity, and they will **not** be held accountable for anything bad they've done—no matter how bad it is, no matter how long they waited to call on Him. They will stand in His presence with a clean slate. *Again, that's the amazing grace of God.* God Himself came from heaven to earth in order to save mankind from their sins for no other reason than the fact that He loves us and wants a relationship with us. God didn't "scrap the project." Because He loves us; He had a plan. This strange plan of God goes against human nature as we know it. We know that mankind is a prideful bunch, and we love to talk about our accomplishments. God's plan, unlike man's, leaves *no* room for man's pride.

I was thinking about this too: What would motivate any man to invent a plan or religion that places himself at the mercy of [a] God? What's in it for man to invent such a plan, a plan that requires the acknowledgment of a higher authority and a complete dependence on Him? What's in it for man to invent a religion in which he gets absolutely no credit for his own victory but gives all credit to a personal power that he made up, called God? Not to mention that he may be persecuted or killed for even saying such things as this. What would inspire anyone to risk his life and invent a plan that serves no one but an imaginary God? The answer is *nothing.* Men like plans that point to themselves, saying, "Look at me; see what I've done!" In God's plan, men are pointing to the cross, saying, "Look at **Jesus**; see what **God** has done!"

There is nothing for anyone to gain by telling you this message. There is nothing for me to gain by telling you the simple message of God: "God so loved the world that He gave His only begotten Son, that whosoever believes in Him should not perish but have eternal life" (John 3:16). This plan of salvation *through Jesus* Christ **alone** is clearly a plan that only the True God, the Creator of the Universe, would have come up with. Why? Because of His deep love for us. Because He wants a relationship with those who **want** a relationship with Him. And like a loving father, God knows and wants what is best for us. Man is too full of himself, too puffed up and egotistical to devise a plan such as this. Yet it is through this amazing and humbling *plan of God* that we are truly lifted up; we finally find *our true sense of self-worth* as we realize that we are loved by God, our very Creator, and that we are totally forgiven by Him. It is only as we humbly recognize and acknowledge our own humanity and its limitations that we are able to realize our full potential and fulfill the true purpose of our life, bringing glory to our Creator as His Spirit transforms us. When I was a little girl, my dad always had a saying for everything, and one thing he used to say to us is this: "You'll get your reward in heaven." He explained to us that we should do nice things just because they're nice, without any expectations of a reward until we get to heaven. When we meet Jesus face-to-face, He will say to us, "Well done!" And you can rest assured that the rewards will be plentiful! "No eye has seen, no ear has heard, no mind has imagined the things that God has *prepared for those who love Him*" (1 Corinthians 2:9). **Jesus** is the answer: *The way,* **The truth** *and The life.* Through His sacrifice on our behalf, we are no longer separated from God by our sins. Instead it is only by humbly accepting our own need of forgiveness that we *become* children of God.

Which leads me to bring up another assumption of a fallen and deceived mankind. I've heard people say this many times throughout my lifetime: "We're all children of God." As nice as that may sound, it is far from the truth. According to the scriptures, the reality is that we are all born as the children of "the god of this world," Satan. We *only* become children of God when we are *spiritually born* into the family of God. Jesus told the Pharisees, "You are of **your** *father, the* **devil**, and your will is to do *your father's* desires. He was a murderer from the beginning, and does *not stand in truth*, because there is no truth in him" (John 8:44). Jesus explained to Nicodemus that in order to enter the Kingdom of heaven, "You must be born again" (John 3:1-21). "The course of *this world* flows in the direction of Satan, who is the 'prince of the power of the air" (Ephesians 2:12). "*The god of this world* has blinded the minds of them who do not believe" (2 Corinthians 4:4). "Now this is the judgement of this world; that *the ruler of this world* will be cast out" (John 12:31). "He has delivered us _from_ the domain of darkness and transferred us _to_ the Kingdom of his beloved Son" (Colossians 1:13). "As many as received Him, _to them_ He gave the right to become children of God, to them that *believe on His name*" (John 1:12). "By this it is evident who are the children of God, and those who are *the children of the devil*; whoever does not practice righteousness is not of God" (John 3:10). "For you are children of God _by faith in Christ Jesus_" (Galatians 3:26).

"I will destroy the wisdom of the wise; the intelligence of the intelligent, I will frustrate." (1 Corinthians 1:19)

## Chapter Twenty-Nine

# NO ONE COMPARES TO JESUS

Perhaps you've never heard any of this unusual, stunning, or what may even sound like outlandish information. By now you may have already labeled me as a Jesus freak or a religious nut, and that's okay. I'll count it all joy. Perhaps this is all news to you, but I pray that it comes as **good news**. Whatever the case may be for you, I urge you to **consider Jesus** and investigate for yourself. If this is your first introduction to Jesus and the Bible, I understand that this may sound like some pretty crazy stuff, yet I have no doubt that every word is true. And my faith continues to grow stronger every day as I grow in the knowledge of God through His word. My sister, Sue shared with me the other day, a statement made by John Loeffler of the News Radio program, Steel on Steel: "Your failure to be informed does not make me a whacko." I laughed as I agreed.

I can assure you that I am not a whacko. The things I have shared with you are certainly *no* more outlandish than to believe, for example, that we will die one day and return in another body or in another form. That sounds pretty crazy to me. Yet people go through life hanging their hat, or resting their eternity, on that belief even though there is **no** evidence to back up such claims that can't be easily refuted by the word of God.

To believe that a higher intelligence such as God as Creator is far less outlandish than to believe that Space + Time + Chance = Something, yet that's the simple conclusion of the Big Bang *theory*; which claims that we're all here in this world by mere chance and *without purpose*. Not to mention the astronomical odds of such an event even happening. As someone put it, "It would be like a tornado going through a junk yard and producing a jumbo jet." What appears to be missing in this theory is the fundamental principle of causation. How do you get something from nothing? Evolutionists will further tell you that we began our existence in a pond of slime, evolving over millions of years from one species to another. Whatever his intent, the science of Darwin's theory has fallen so flat that many in the scientific world have abandoned it completely. Many scientists have found with certainty that Darwin failed to prove any such thing, having found **not** a single piece of evidence to support transitional forms of life through evolution. But rather, *just as God said* in His Word thousands of years ago regarding the species of the earth: "Each bringing forth *after their own kind*" (Genesis 1:24). Simply put, each species may evolve, and in fact *has* evolved, **within** its own species based on various environmental circumstances, but they have *not* evolved from one species to another, and scientists now recognize and admit that openly. This unproven, scientifically baseless *theory* of evolution has been taught as scientific fact in schools for the past fifty years or so. They've indoctrinated a generation of children to believe that they had apes swinging from their family tree at some point. Any theory including fossil dating, claiming our world to be millions or billions of years old is only as good as the assumptions they're built on, and many scientists refute those very assumptions. But you can be sure you won't hear this on the Smithsonian channel or in your public schools. Scientists teaching from the foundations of Darwin and others like him don't have undisputed proof of their theories, but that hasn't stopped them from teaching it to our children in our schools as if they do. This teaching by design, has not only completely undermined the *morality* of the biblical foundations that were taught in previous generations, it has devalued each child teaching them that they came from nothing or a pond of slime, rather than the truth: that they are someone who was perfectly and wonderfully made by God. All of which explains a lot about the moral condition of our world today. If we're all here by mere chance and have no purpose, that also leaves us with no moral standard to speak of. It's "anything goes!" The devil's been hard at work and as we look around, he appears to be winning. Thankfully, we know that God will prevail and the devil will be put in His place, in God's perfect time; and that time is right around the corner.

This information I'm offering you is no more outlandish than to say that all roads, all beliefs, will land you in heaven simply because *you* believe it. That makes absolutely no sense, not to mention it sounds arrogant and careless to me. This message is also no more outlandish than to believe that we will simply cease to exist: that we are born into this world; spend a specific period of time here, develop and nurture relationships, go through countless trials; experience extraordinary, remarkable, and memorable events and joyous milestones—learning and growing in knowledge and wisdom—just to have it come to an abrupt end, to be placed in the ground, and then to be covered up with a mound of dirt. That, to me sounds extremely bleak, purposeless and highly unlikely.

It seems that many of the world's most brilliant minds have gone to great extremes to try to disprove the existence of a higher intelligence such as God, and surely they're frustrated, because it simply can't be done. Their hatred toward God is blatant. Some world-renowned geniuses have gone to their own graves proclaiming, "There is no God." They spent their God-given gifts, their intellect, their talents, and their entire lives, even to their own end, shaking their fists at God. Surely they have a change of tune now while their spirit, their eternal consciousness lies in awareness of what is to come, as they await their own eternal judgment from the very God they refused to even acknowledge let alone pay homage to. They may be thinking about all the opportunities they had, to come to the true and living God through faith in His beloved Son, Jesus. And likely, because of their hardened hearts, they will still be shaking their fists at God—because of their decision, knowing now that instead of gathering at the throne of grace, they will be brought before God at the throne of wrath. There, they will be judged for eternity because they chose not to believe that Jesus had paid the *necessary* price to save them from their sins; they will now pay the price themselves. (Romans 6:23) They thought they were so smart, *and they were*, but their own pride stood between them and the living God. "I will destroy the wisdom of the wise; the intelligence of the intelligent, I will frustrate" (1 Corinthians 3:19).

On the other hand, there are plenty of other equally brilliant minds who have no problem seeing the hand of God in the very intricacies of all creation. The world-renowned genius Stephen Hawking, although he couldn't prove that there was no God, claims to have proven that a higher intelligence such as God was not necessary for the universe to exist. To that, another world-renowned genius, John Lennox refuted his claim and responded with this: "Nonsense remains nonsense, even when talked about by world-famous scientists." There are many others of their intellectual status that share those sentiments. Clearly this subject is not a matter of intellect; it's a matter of the heart.

I always find this interesting: People go through life accepting all kinds of beliefs in spite of faulty, questionable, or half-baked ideas, with little or no proof. Yet when it comes to the God of the Bible—the Creator and Savior—they insist on absolute proof. This fact alone makes it pretty clear to me that there's more to people's rejection of Jesus than they may be willing to admit. It all boils down to one thing: pride. They don't seem to be really looking for **truth** or proof, but rather it appears they're looking to embrace an eternal plan that fits their own personal preferences for their lifestyle today; they may not like submission to, or acknowledgment of, the true, living God because it simply doesn't suit them. It's like the guy sitting with his shopping cart full of stuff on the side of the road: he doesn't really *want* to change his life. He's *fine* right where he is and will be okay just to make it through the rest of the day. People may reject the gospel for the same reason: they may be unwilling and reluctant to accept Jesus, thinking that God might want them to change something. Well, I admit, they would be right about that. Although Christianity is not about being "religious," *His truth* is sure to challenge you, and undoubtedly His Holy Spirit will change you. But you can also be sure that if the Spirit of God has His way, you will be the best version of yourself. You will be what you were born to be. It's inevitable. But most aren't up for a challenge or a change; they are full of pride and want to be the shot-caller of their own life. Who knows? Perhaps the empty promise of Satan "You can be like God" may be running through their head. They still don't get it, try as they might; they will never be like God while they are in rebellion against Him. Ultimately they will suffer eternal judgment because of that rebellion.

In God's plan, when it comes to where you'll spend eternity the only shot God allows us to call is to accept his offer or reject it. Like the old saying, "You can take it or leave it." The bottom line is this: I can't prove to you that there **is** a God, that He created the whole world, and everything in it. I can't prove that He loves you so much that He sent His beloved Son, Jesus to save you and the entire world from their sins, any more than an atheist can prove otherwise; although they've gone to great lengths to do so. That's where faith comes in, and as I said, *everyone* has faith in something. While I can't offer you absolute proof of **God**, in Jesus we have solid evidence **of Him**—not based on myths and fables but on facts recorded in history, through firsthand accounts that are unrefuted by both secular and non-secular historical scholars. Yes, the historically recorded facts about Jesus are extraordinary, but that's actually the point. If Jesus were an ordinary guy who did ordinary things, His name would likely have died on the cross right along with Him. His resurrection from life to death *sets Him apart* and changed everything. Christianity is fundamentally dependent on historical *facts* that have stood the test of time. Along with its *historical accuracy*, it is overflowing with spiritual truths that are multidimensional and transcend all generations, and they have stood the test of time as well.

There is *no one* who can compare to **Jesus**, and in fact, no one even comes close. Jesus is a historical figure. His life, ministry, death, and resurrection were all recorded by firsthand witnesses who had nothing to gain by their testimony of Him except perhaps their own persecution or death. Other religions and philosophies of the world have nothing and no one solid to rest their claims on, and they offer **no hope** for mankind. However, the more I investigate and study God's word, the more I understand the plan of God. There are solid answers for everything regarding our lives here on earth as well as answers about the earth itself, as God runs circles around *science*. I can see the fulfilled prophecies written thousands of years prior to the events, concerning the birth, the life, and the death of Jesus, and I continue to see prophecy being fulfilled in our generation with precise accuracy. The best evidence I can offer is the changed hearts and the testimonies of those who have placed their faith in the gospel of Christ. Because the Spirit of God gives special insight through His written word, I can see the pieces of life's puzzle coming together with amazing clarity. I find hope in **Jesus** and His promises, **not** because they make me *feel* good, although they surely do, but because His accomplishments have validated His claims. His works are a part of our history and have also offered hope for our future. My prayer is that you will consider these things, as outlandish, outrageous or preposterous as they may sound to you. When all is said and done, there will be **the *truth***, and there will be everything else. **Only the *truth* will stand.** As narrow-minded as that may sound, when it comes to these *matters of truth* and eternity, everyone can't be right.

"Remember the former of old. For I am God and there is no other. I am God and there is none like Me. Declaring the end from the beginning. And **foretelling from ancient times** things that are not yet done. My counsel shall stand... I will also bring it to pass. I have purposed it; **I will also do it**." (Isaiah 46:9-11)

## *Chapter Thirty*

## LIVING IN EXCITING TIMES

What I've shared with you here today is merely the tip of the iceberg. The scriptures are rich and overflowing with the answers to life's questions, from its origin to its ending, a treasure trove of jewels and gems—alive, full of wisdom and truth. Likely there are still plenty of "What about this?" and "What about that?" questions that people may have. And I will always welcome the opportunity to discuss them with anyone who is truly interested. Although as I said, at times questions are asked as a diversion with no real desire for an answer, I assure you *God has answers for every question*. Most importantly He has revealed enough for us to gain salvation and eternal life through His only begotten Son,

Jesus, and when we see Him face-to-face, we can ask Him anything we like. "For now we see dimly as in a mirror *but then face to face*" (1 Corinthians 13:12). The second coming of Jesus Christ to earth has been promised throughout both Old and New Testament scripture: "Behold, He is coming with the clouds, and every eye will see Him – even those who pierced Him. And all the tribes of the earth will mourn because of Him. So shall it be! Amen. (Revelation 1:7) We are living in exciting times. In scripture, Jesus's return has been referred to as "the great and terrible day of the Lord." or "the great and dreadful day of the Lord." (Joel 2:31, Malachi 4:5). Although not the accurate translation of the word *great* in these verses, I always think of this when I read them: one thing is certain, that day will be "great" for some, but no doubt "terrible and dreadful" for those who are still here during that time.

God has foretold us everything: "Remember the former of old. For I am God and there is no other. I am God and there is none like Me. Declaring the end from the beginning. And *foretelling from ancient times* things that are not yet done. My counsel shall stand.... I will also bring it to pass. I have purposed it; *I will also do it*" (Isaiah 46:9–11). Just as every prophecy written in the thousands of years leading up to the birth of Jesus had been fulfilled with amazing and precise exactness, we can see the *end-time* prophecies leading to the great and terrible Day of the Lord being fulfilled as I write these words. Although there are many prophetical signs of Jesus's soon return, one of the most prominent signs is the moral condition of the world today. Looking through the lens of prophecy, there's no doubt that the time is ripe for Jesus's return. Jesus warned: "as the days of Noah were, so shall also be the coming of the Son of Man." (Luke 17:26). In those days, with the exception of Noah and his family who loved and walked closely with God, the entire population had removed God from their lives, allowing Satan and his demons to take over; resulting in rampant moral depravity and evil of every kind. The interesting thing is that as pure evil consumed the world during those days, they were so spiritually blinded that they didn't even recognize it as evil, it didn't seem to bother any of them. They continued on eating, drinking and marrying and so on.–*but it bothered God*. It bothered Him so much that they were completely destroyed from the face of the earth. God had the final word then and He will have the final word when He returns at the end of this age. You don't have to ask, "Are we there yet?" As I look at our world today, completely unphased at the evil condition of the world; eating drinking, marrying, and many cases celebrating the evil itself; there's no doubt we've arrived! Yes, we're here, just as it was in the days of Noah. And just like in those days, with the exception of the few, the remnant who love God and walk with Him, evil doesn't seem to bother anyone.

For the past several decades there has been a steady down shift of morality; as the world has turned its back on God, evil and good have been redefined. While the world is at the brink of a moral collapse, people are in such a state of spiritual darkness that they can't even see it happening right before their eyes. They are either oblivious to or perfectly happy with the direction the world is heading, just like those who had turned from God in the days of Noah. People are deceiving themselves while our world is spiraling out of control all in the name of *tolerance*. This is just *one of many* examples of where our world is headed: we live in a world where boys can be girls, and girls can be boys, they can change their minds whenever they want to according to whatever they may *identify as,* from one day to another. And if they don't like either, they can choose from an assortment of various genders. What's next!? Forty some years ago when my first son was about two or three years old, I remember one day he *identified as a puppy.* It was actually very cute. But thankfully for him, I didn't put a bowl of kibble down on the floor, and open the back door for him to relieve himself in order to *validate his feelings.* One of my daughters has been a Sign Language Interpreter for deaf children for several years at the Irvine Unified School district in California. This year before the school began their new semester, she along with the other teachers and staff members were instructed on political correctness to avoid *offending* anyone; they were cautioned as to particular words *not to use* when referring to their students: "don't say boys, or girls, don't say he or she, don't say him or her" and so on. And the people behind this are the very people who call Christians "science deniers." It feels like I'm living in "bizzarro world." Everything is up-side-down and backwards these days. It's God who has *no tolerance* for such nonsense, and He will have the last word. "Woe to those who call evil good and good evil, who turn

118

darkness to light and light to darkness, who replace bitter with sweet and sweet with bitter. Woe to those who are wise in their own eyes and clever in their own sight." (Isaiah 5:20-21). That's a lot of woes! The dictionary definitions for the word "woe," range from misery and sorrow to catastrophe and calamity.

Until that day when God sets things straight, I can write or talk till I'm blue in the face about the wonders and majesty of Jesus, share with you all kinds of evidence and logic and so on, but it's only through the miraculous work of the Spirit of God that we gain any understanding at all. "For the natural man does not accept the things of the Spirit of God, for they are foolishness to him; and he cannot understand them because they are spiritually appraised" (1 Corinthians 2:14). This is what the bible tells us: We are chosen before the foundations of the earth, we are *drawn* by the Father, and we are *saved* by faith in His only begotten Son, Jesus, and *transformed* through the working of the Holy Spirit of God. Which in and of itself is a mystery of God and may sound like a lot of foolishness, but nonetheless it's *the truth*. I think of it like this: I don't know anyone who insists on understanding all of the mechanics or innerworkings of their various devices, before they push the "power" button and begin their day. Through His written word, God has given us all we need to know to be saved, more than enough to push the *power* button, so to speak, by placing our faith in Him. Jesus said that we need to have the faith of *a child* to enter the Kingdom of Heaven. It is pure arrogance of a rebellious mankind to expect or assume that we should or would understand the entirety of the vast knowledge, and intricate calculations of God, the Creator of the Universe before we can trust Him. We have been given everything we need in His word and His creation which surrounds us. The word of God will be received in one of two ways by those who hear it. "For the message of the cross is foolishness to those who perish, but to those who are saved, it is the *power of God*" (1 Corinthians 1:18). The apostle Paul boldly proclaims this: "For I am not ashamed of the gospel of Christ, for it is *the power of God* unto salvation" (Romans 1:16). Those who have placed their faith in Jesus have no need to fear that great and terrible day of the Lord. Instead, they will find comfort and shelter, and can rest easy in the love and grace of God. For believers it will be a "great" day indeed! Jesus will be like the ark was to Noah and His family when the time comes for His final judgement.

Today we're living in a world where we are actually watching biblical *prophecy* become biblical *history* before our eyes, and I believe that the time of the Lord's return is at hand; I'm not setting dates but watching the signs that we've been encouraged to look for. I'll just say that it's right around the corner. In my attempts to share this information with those I love, I have been rebuffed by some. It seems that they had entirely missed the point or misunderstood; I am extremely aware that nothing I do can change God's timing. Rather I'm very excited because I see that things appear to be moving along rapidly and in line with biblical prophecy whether I happen to like it or not. Naturally, out of a heart of love, I want to tell people because I don't want anyone to be caught off guard and taken by surprise, especially my own family and friends.

When talking to non-Christians about the gospel of Jesus or end-time events—although not always the case—I almost expect to hear skeptical, dismissive, or patronizing responses. But I was very disheartened after talking to someone I've always considered a dear Christian friend about what I referred to as "the exciting times we're living in" and the biblical, prophetical implications. I naturally assumed she would be excited or at least interested to hear that the *possibility* that the return of Jesus could be sooner than we think. Instead she sounded apprehensive about the whole idea of Jesus coming back soon, especially considering that the rapture of the church precedes His second coming. Her response caught me by surprise. She didn't deny the scriptural claims of the rapture or the return of Jesus. However, I found that she wasn't looking forward to it with any amount of excitement or anticipation. In fact, her response was the exact opposite. The next day she suggested that I may be trying to "rush things along." Going back to the word of God, I realized that my perspective was the biblical perspective, so I didn't let it get me down. In fact, I was more encouraged and determined than ever to share the message of the gospel and the grace of God as I read these words from the apostle Peter:

"But the day of the Lord will come as a thief in the night, in which the heavens will pass away with a great noise, and the elements will melt with fervent heat; Therefore, since all these things will be dissolved, what manner of person ought you to be, in holy conduct and godliness, *looking for and hastening* the coming of the day of God, because of which the heavens will be dissolved being on fire, and the elements will melt with fervent heat? Nevertheless we, according to His promise, *look for* the new heavens and a new earth in which righteousness dwells. Therefore, beloved *looking forward to* these things, be diligent to be found by Him in peace without spot and blameless." (2 Peter 3:10–14). Thankfully, although I was a little down after hearing her response, the word of God confirmed that I had the right perspective and that was comforting to know.

The issue for me wasn't whether I was right or wrong about the prospect of the soon return of Jesus, but rather my disappointment was that it seemed that she was hoping that I was wrong, that Jesus's return would wait a while. "Wait for what, I thought? What could be better news for a Christian? As we talked that night, she indicated that she was hoping Jesus wouldn't be coming anytime soon; she said that she was hoping it would be "like maybe a hundred years from now." She didn't want to miss out on various family events and milestones regarding her children and grandchildren. As it turned out, instead of having someone to share in my interest and excitement about the subject of biblical prophecy, I felt as if I had just rained on her parade.

She didn't sound the least bit happy, let alone excited. I completely understand her deep love for her family and her sense of peace in her blessed life and so on. I have a family that I love deeply too. Although I look forward to the milestones and the successes of my own children and grandchildren, when I place *all of those things*—as wonderful as they are—on one side of a scale and then place *being in heaven with Jesus, the Eternal Son of God, the Savior of the world, giver of eternal life, and so on*, on the other side of that scale, the side holding Jesus far outweighs them all. In my mind Jesus *far* outweighs anything else you can place on the other side of that scale. Beyond that, outside of our own personal bubble of life that we each may live in, as we consider the grim condition of the world as a whole today, and as we look back at the wars and struggles of mankind throughout recorded history, what could be better than living in a perfect world with Jesus, the perfect Son of God, reigning as King? And ultimately, I realize that God's timing is not in my hands.

Anyway, apparently even some within the church these days, are comfortably wrapped up in their own world, living in a bubble of sorts; they say their prayers, go to church, read their Bibles, and so on, and for various reasons, they are very comfortable keeping the return of Jesus somewhere in the *far-off distance*. Perhaps because it's been that way for so long, I don't know. But if you are truly a Christian, it's time to wake up and realize that this generation is far different than any other before. Sadly, they don't seem to be looking for *the signs* that Jesus Himself said to look for, and even sadder, they don't seem to want to hear about it or even think about it. I continue to pray for my friend and for the many others who may tell you without hesitation that they love the Lord, but you realize when you talk about the likelihood or even the *possibility* of the end-times, and particularly the rapture approaching, that they aren't quite ready to let go of this world. And like my friend, they're hoping maybe in "like a hundred years from now." That puzzles me, but more than that, it concerns me because I don't want anyone to be unprepared, to be so *caught up in the world* that His coming would surprise them as a thief in the night. Jesus gave this warning to those who are clinging too tightly to their worldly lives: He said "Remember Lot's wife. Whosoever seeks to keep his life will lose it, and whosoever will lose his life will preserve it." (Luke 17:32). To refresh your memory: it was Lot's wife, who along with her family, was instructed to escape the devastation that was about to come, to flee the city *and don't look back*. However, she was *so attached* to the life she had there, and in spite of the instruction and warning; revealing the condition of her heart, she couldn't resist looking back at all she was leaving behind. She was clinging too tightly and she lost her life. That was the example that Jesus Himself used. Those earlier verses that I just referenced from the apostle, Peter, said to us three times in different ways that we are to be prepared, to be watching and waiting: "*looking for* and *hastening* the coming of the day of God, *look for* the new heavens and a new earth, Therefore, beloved *looking forward* to these things" Those and so many other verses throughout scripture that give us that same advice. I think taking that advice helps us to live life here with the proper perspective and enhances our spiritual walk until He returns for us.

So whether it be a hundred years from now or sooner, I don't know, but I can't help but look forward to it as I see prophecy being fulfilled.

In knowing that Jesus's return *could*, and may very well be soon coming, perhaps even in this very generation, I pray that other Christians will **draw closer to Him, sanctify themselves**, and trust in the sovereignty of God as they prepare to meet Him. I also think of the words of the apostle John. "And now little children, abide in Him, that *when He appears*, we may have confidence and *not be ashamed before Him at His coming*" (1 John 2:28). In light of what I know, I'm certainly not *rushing anything*, but I'm not ignoring the obvious either.

Meanwhile I continue on each day that I'm here with focus and purpose. I realize that even with some of my own children and family, "you can lead a horse to water, but you can't make them drink." In that, I trust in the sovereignty of God; I continue to pray for them and so many others, I try to make the most of my opportunities, and to continue to share the love of God through the gospel of Jesus. I don't cling too tightly to this world, because as we all know; our life can end in a moment's time, but I am so thankful and enjoy the blessings I've been given while I'm here: I am a mother of seven, and I love my children deeply, and I love all of my wonderful, precious grandchildren. I have the sweetest husband in the world and the most wonderful family and friends anyone could ask for. I have birthdays, graduations, weddings, road trips, Holidays, which I especially love, and other exciting events on my calendar that I'm really looking forward to. At the same time, along with the rest of the world, I am dealing with the daily struggles and tragedies of life. But whatever my situation, I understand that *God's appointed times* are preordained from eternity, and I don't assume that they were determined around my life or calendar of events. Another thing to remember, and I encouraged my friend with this as well: we will have an eternity of exciting events to plan and to look forward to in the Kingdom of God. Meanwhile we should do our best while we're here, to share this truth with as many as possible. As for the events we'll be planning in heaven, I'll say, "the more, the merrier!"

I'm praying that the gospel of God's Amazing Grace will continue to reach many throughout the world and that Christians get excited and that their faith is reignited, that they *wake up* to see the signs that have been set before us, foretold thousands of years ago for a generation far in the future. It looks as though we could be that very generation. I pray that they will see that the time of the Lord's return may be closer than we might have thought, and praying that they too will be "*Looking for* the Blessed Hope and the glorious appearing of our Great God and Savior Jesus Christ" (Titus 2:13). Meanwhile, with each day I'm given, I continue to try to be a light in the darkness, though I feel very alone in my faith much of the time. As I told my friend, "I feel like I'm jumping for joy all by myself." I realize more and more each day that I am a foreigner, an alien in this world, even among most of my family and friends. But thankfully, "The Joy of the Lord is my Strength." The more I see the condition of the world today, the uncertainty of life itself, as we live in the shadows of things to come, the more I look forward to living in a world where a perfect, holy God is in charge, where we will see Jesus face-to-face. He will wipe away every tear, there will be no more sorrow or death, where the old things have passed away, and **all things will be made new**. Nothing in this world will compare to that, and I believe it's so close we can almost touch it.

"The coming of the lawless one is according to the work of Satan, with all power, signs and lying wonders, and with all unrighteous deception among those who perish, *because* they did not receive *the love of the truth* that they might be saved." (1 Thessalonians 2:9-10)

## Chapter Thirty One

# THE TWINKLING OF AN EYE, A STRONG DELUSION AND THE FINAL SHOWDOWN

I mentioned in the Introduction of this book, that *barring a divine intervention*, no one is excluded from death. For Christians that divine intervention is referred to as "the blessed hope" and commonly known as *the rapture*. I touched on the subject in the previous chapter as well. So what is the rapture? I will preface this explanation by admitting that this thing we know as the rapture may *sound* preposterous even to those eschatology scholars who confidently and extensively teach on the subject. However, they have no doubt that the rapture as taught throughout scripture, is absolutely true, and going to happen *exactly* as it is written. Okay, so let's talk about this seemingly preposterous event: The rapture refers to believers in the last generation of mankind who will be delivered and sheltered from the *wrath* to come and will *not* face death; the wrath which was described by the apostle, Peter in the last chapter, where the earth will melt with intense heat and so on as well as many other verses describing the various and horrific judgements that will befall the world. The believers who are still alive, in the midst of various places and activities will be taken up into heaven miraculously and instantaneously. Also in an instant, just before—though almost simultaneously—the resurrection of all the believers who have died, from every generation will take place. This event will happen prior to the tribulation that will come upon the world during the last generation and prior to the second coming of Jesus Christ to earth. As preposterous as that may *sound*, when I look at *mankind's* incredible technology of today; I realize how preposterous the digital world we live in today sounded just fifty to a hundred years ago. Now think how much more advanced God, the Creator's *unlimited abilities* are than those of mankind, the creation's, with all of our limitations. When you consider the vast difference between God and man, the rapture is sounding less and less preposterous by the minute. Point being: If you believe in God, as He has revealed Himself, nothing is preposterous or impossible for Him. After all, He is God. The question isn't so much whether or not you believe in the rapture, but whether or not you believe in the God of the Bible. Anyway, although the word *rapture* is not found in the Bible, the concept of its teaching is throughout scripture. *Rapture* is a word that comes from the Latin word *rapturo* or the Greek word *harpazo*, both translated as: a transport, a snatching away, to take possession of, to be taken by force, which is spoken of throughout the Bible. This is what Christians have looked forward to since the inception of the gospel of Christ; you might say it is kind of like the *Grand finale* or the epic crescendo for believers during this *dispensational age of grace* that we're in now.

The early believers understood the immanency of this event and looked forward to it with great anticipation *even then*. Believers today do even more so, as we come to the end of the age. There is a group of believers, those of the *last* generation of mankind on this earth, who will not experience physical death, who will be snatched away in an instant; they will be miraculously taken up into heaven, personally escorted by Jesus Himself. Wow! They will be sheltered and protected by Him from the catastrophic events that will take place on the earth during the time of the great tribulation. "For then there will be great distress, unequaled from the beginning of the world until **now—and** *never to be equaled again. If those days* are not cut short, no one would survive, but for the sake of *the elect* those days will be shortened" (Matthew 24:21–23). In other words, the end of the world. Many scholars of eschatology, those who study end-time prophecy, believe it is coming upon us more quickly than you might have thought, if you even thought of it at all. In any case, Christians from all generations, past and present—whether they're to be raptured or have died—have been given the comfort of knowing they will be safe with their Savior during that terrible time of wrath and judgment known as the Great Tribulation.

This is the opinion of many biblical, prophetic scholars, and I tend to agree. In light of the current events unfolding throughout the world, we can see biblical prophecy coming to pass before our eyes, and see that time is drawing closer to the Second Coming of Jesus Christ, which we know takes place at the end of the seven-year tribulation period, that will be the last seven years of human history on this earth. Anyway, according to scripture, the rapture of the Church **will precede** this terrible time and the believers *will not be here* during that period of time. This period is also known scripturally as "the time of Jacob's trouble," because although it will affect the entire planet, ultimately it is meant for the judgment of the Nation of Israel and *not for the church*. Contrary to the teaching of many, God has not forsaken His chosen people, the Jews. He has a special plan for the Nation of Israel which will be accomplished through this time of the great tribulation. "The church" refers to the believers of today as well as past generations. We don't know how much of a lapse of time there will be before the great tribulation period begins, after the rapture takes place, if any; whether it will be immediate or a few years, we don't know, and opinions may slightly vary, but most biblical scholars assume it will be a relatively short period of time according to the prophetic implications. Jesus promised that He would personally receive us to Himself. This is a very different event than the second coming of Jesus to earth when He will be coming in full fury and judgement. He is going to take the church, which He lovingly refers to as *His bride*, to a place of safety during that time. "Let not your hearts be troubled; you believe in God, believe also in me. In My Father's house are many mansions; If it were not so, I would have told you. I go to prepare a place for you. And if I go and prepare a place for you, I will come again and *receive you to Myself*; that where I am there you may also be." (John 14:1-3). He is going to personally come for us. "For the Lord Himself will descend from heaven with a shout with the voice of an archangel, and with the trumpet of God. And the dead in Christ will rise first. Then those who are alive and remain shall be caught up together with them in the clouds to meet the Lord in the air. And thus we shall always be with the Lord. Therefore comfort one another with these words." (1 Thessalonians 4: 16-18). "No one knows the day or the hour."(Mark 13:32) But it will take place in an instant: "In a moment, in the twinkling of an eye, at the last trumpet: for the trumpet shall sound, and the dead shall be raised incorruptible, and we who are alive shall be changed" (1 Corinthians 15:52).

Anyway, as you can imagine, when the rapture does take place, when those who belong to God are safely removed from the planet, naturally the whole world will be in an uproar; there will be utter confusion and chaos. It will be an event unlike anything the world has ever experienced. You can be sure people everywhere will be frantic, wondering what the heck is going on, when millions of people suddenly and mysteriously disappear from various places in the midst of various activities from one end of the planet to the other, leaving a path of confusion and destruction. I believe that the groundwork is already laid and a plausible narrative is already in place for this event to be successfully explained away. Keep in mind: **Satan knows the scriptures too**. Remember, he used them and perverted them in his failed attempt to temp Jesus in the wilderness; he quoted directly from the Old Testament, book of Psalms. (Matthew 4:1-11). And as I said, Satan knows full well that his time is running short: "Therefore rejoice, you heavens and you who dwell in them! But *woe to the inhabitants of the earth* and the sea, because the devil has gone down to you! He is filled with fury, *because he knows that his time is short.*" (Revelation 12:12). And knowing that, Satan is making the necessary preparations for the *greatest deception of all* that will take place shortly before Jesus's return, and the real-life, ultimate battle between good and evil that will take place right here on earth–the *final showdown* between GOD and Satan!

I'd like to offer one *consideration* for the explanation that may be given after the rapture takes place: You may have noticed the growing interest in paranormal activity and particularly aliens in the past several decades. From television sitcoms with loveable alien characters like Alph or Mork from the planet Ork, to the big screen with movies like Star Wars, Close Encounters, ET, Men in Black and hundreds of others. Until recently, the world's been *subtly* conditioned to the idea of UFOs and aliens. Although the well-known event in Roswell, New Mexico took place in 1947 the Government brushed it under the rug, labeling those who questioned them, *conspiracy theorists*. From then till now, Satan was at work, getting all his ducks in a row, all of his useful idiots in place; finally it *appears* that the powers that be are fully cooperating and have decided *now is the time* to reveal previously classified "UFO and alien" information to the public. The number of "UFO sightings and alien activity" reports have spiked dramatically. The Pentagon recently released videos of unknown spacecraft, capturing the attention of many, adding to this piqued interest in aliens. It is all a part of Satan's deceptive plan: the necessary, psychological conditioning in order to explain away the rapture when it happens; to get people looking to anything but God when millions of people vanish from the earth. Remember Satan's mission is to *keep people from the truth.*

Here are just a few examples of hundreds of recent reports regarding aliens and UFOs: USA Today–July 29, 2020, "In 2020 anything is possible. New government intelligence might prove alien life is too..." CNN–August 13, 2020, "The Pentagon is forming a new task force to investigate UFOs..." New York Times – July 2020, "No longer in the shadows, Pentagon's UFO Unit will make some findings public." Jerusalem Post – December 5, 2020 "Professor Haim Eshed who served from 1981-2010 as the head of Israel's security space program and over the years received the Israel Security award three times, twice for *confidential technological inventions* said this: 'The UFOs have asked not to publish that they are here, humanity is not ready yet. Trump was on the verge of revealing, but the aliens in the Galactic Federation are saying: 'Wait, let people calm down first. They don't want to start mass hysteria. They want to first make us sane and understanding.'" Even more recently, written into the latest COVID-19 stimulus package was the promise to disclose classified UFO information within the next 180 days. The conditioning now is *no longer subtle*; it's no longer just in fictional movies and light-hearted sitcoms. The open talk of UFOs and aliens is now being touted by government officials and mainstream media outlets. Satan knows exactly what he's doing. Many have already credited the *rapid advancement of technology* in the past several decades to aliens. I believe they aren't far off. I don't dismiss, deny or doubt sightings, reports, and stories of aliens and alien abduction; however, I believe that all this *strange activity* is nothing less than **demonic activity** coordinated by Satan himself. His power is only second to God's, and *deception* is Satan's middle name. Remember the bible warns us that we wrestle NOT against flesh and blood, but against demons and the dark powers of this world. We are getting a lot of help with our special advanced technology from those, whether knowingly or not, who are under direct demonic influences, and they have a grand and *evil agenda*. You can be sure Satan and his demonic minions have been preparing for, and have long awaited this time. The Roswell event occurred in 1947, during which time the preparations for the Jewish people to reclaim their homeland, Israel was taking place. As I mentioned, Satan is well aware from the scriptures that the Jews would be back in Israel in the last days, just prior to Jesus's second coming. Satan knew his time clock was ticking fast as he realized that the Jewish people were about to reclaim their land, which happened less than a year later! He had to come up with something, and boy did he! He also knows that the *final show down* of the entire world's history takes place in Israel, and he is well aware that according to scripture, he is the LOSER! Satan has seen his fate written in stone for thousands of years and he knows he's going down. However, EVIL continues to be himself, the father of lies will continue to deceive even himself and will stop at nothing; he still has a couple of moves left, and he isn't giving up or going down without a fight. But make no mistake, he IS going down.

This mass disappearance will very likely be explained away by media outlets as an *alien abduction*. That explanation will be fully endorsed by the ever popular and growing New Age movement—possibly claiming it to be a necessary *cleansing of the planet* from those not "enlightened" enough, like those pesky, backward Christians who are holding back the world's enlightenment and progression. You can check out the New Age websites to see this very message being perpetuated on a regular basis. Remember we've been warned that Satan and his multitude of demons can manifest in any form, even as an angel of light, so I don't put anything past them. They're crafty little devils. The scientists, geniuses, and techies of the world may offer lofty explanations of quantum physics and things of that nature as well. What we are experiencing in the world now is a foreshadow of the "strong delusion" that God foretold of, that will come about in the last days.

Anyway, that was just one plausible consideration, but whatever the explanation, as you'd expect, this unprecedented rapture event will trigger a domino effect of world events. None of this should come as a surprise to Christians who have paid attention to eschatology. The world is already being *set up* and we are being *psychologically conditioned* for the globalist system as well, the New World Order, One World Government, digital currency, and so on, which has all been *foretold thousands of years ago* and laid out in the Book of Revelation as well as through many other Old Testament prophecies. The powers that be have been working toward this one cause and are driven by *demonic* forces, and they will bring a drastic change to the world order. They will usher in a new world leader along with his religious sidekick. They're all hard at work behind the scenes as we speak. We don't know for certain who this new leader will be, as were told in the scriptures that he will **not** be *revealed* until the church has been removed. There are many possibilities in the world today who fit the bill. This new world leader will be greeted by most, like a breath of fresh air; he will be the one to make order out of chaos. He will come onto the scene at just the right time, as the man with the plan, a smooth-talking guy who is going to fix everything! Of course the masses left behind may not realize right away that their new charismatic hero is the *Antichrist*, referred to in the scriptures among other things, as *the beast*. He's been empowered by, and has fully given himself over to, none other than Satan himself!

The technology is already available for this new leader to implement what many know of as the *mark of the beast*, spoken of in the book of revelation. It's remarkable to think how far and more so, *how fast* technology is developing; literally changing by the day, so much that it's hard to keep up with the newest thing. Don't you find it interesting that for the thousands of years prior to 1864 when *the first train* became the new fast paced reality for travelers, mankind had counted on the likes of camels, horses, covered wagons and as my dad used to call it, "the shoe leather express" which meant walking, to get from place to place? And to think that the *modern* form of communication back then, was the telegram. That was just over a hundred-fifty years ago! Here we are today, sending rockets to the moon and living in a fully automated, digital world of satellites, transmitters and transponders and nearly instant gratification in travel and communication.

As we can see, the technology for this *mark of the beast*, is locked and loaded. "He required everyone- small and great, rich and poor, free and slave, to receive a mark on the right hand or on the forehead. And no one could buy or sell anything without that mark, which was either the name of the beast or the number representing his name. Here is wisdom. Let him who has understanding calculate the number of the beast, for the number is six hundred, sixty-six." (Revelation 13:18) Interestingly or nefariously enough, a bill was introduced to the House of Congress on May 1, 2020. The name of the Bill is–H.R. 6666 in response to COVID-19. It's for **T**esting, **R**esearching, **A**nd **C**ontacting **E**veryone, and it's known by its acronym name as the TRACE act. I am *not* saying that this tracking system is the "mark of the beast," however, this bill being introduced is just one of many examples showing the direction in which we're heading. The idea is to be able to *track* everyone on the planet and now with COVID-19, they have a "reasonable" excuse to do just that. Satan knows exactly what he's doing and whether those in power realize it or not, although I believe that some do, this is all working towards what the scriptures have foretold, written more than two thousand years ago. The technology is here and at no other time in history could this have been a reality, but thanks to the extreme and rapid advancement of technology, it's all ready to go and be implemented at the *right* time. Many are already talking about replacing currency with digital chips and implants and so on; the information on this subject is readily available and being touted openly. This system of *the anti-Christ* is at the door.

This new leader's religious sidekick is known in scriptures as the *false prophet*. This false prophet will bring about The One World Religion, which appears at this point to be all-inclusive. This ecumenical One World Religion will embrace all religions and all gods. I have to say from what I've seen, Pope Francis is an excellent prototype for whoever steps into this position, if he doesn't fill it himself. He's surely mastered the art of deception, he has *a way with words*, and knows how to manipulate the masses; *portraying* himself as a humble "man of the people" kind of guy. He is a true depiction of the wolf in sheep's clothing that the bible sternly warns of. "Beware of false prophets, which come to you in sheep's clothing, but inwardly they are ravening wolves." (Matthew 7:15) Aside from making multiple shocking, public statements in *blatant opposition* to biblical teaching going back as far as 2013, in recent years his clear demonic possession has become more and more obvious, speaking words that come from the very pit of hell. Yet they're very seductive to the masses, including some of those in the Catholic Church, who unwittingly may be following his every word. Pope Francis has led all the religious leaders in the signing of a Unity Declaration, agreeing that they *all unite as one*, whether Muslims, Christians, Jews, Buddhists, whatever god you choose, coming together in "love," leaving all differences behind and he continues his drum beat of *unity*. It all *sounds* so tolerant and so nice. Even more recently the pope has weighed in on climate change and issues of social inequality, keeping in line with the world's religions of humanism. Leave it to the devil to come up with such a peaceful, tolerant, all-inclusive *religious package* while he leads his victims subtly into the lake of fire. Satan is a master **deceiver**: he knows how to market deception, but he knows nothing about love or truth, other than to imitate it for the purpose of evil. He is the very essence of evil, and he hates the truth. Remember, his number-one job is to keep people *from* the truth. Thankfully, I've heard that there are many Catholics now who have recognized that their leader is a dangerous and false prophet and have turned to Jesus, the way, the truth and the life.

Christians who know the word of God haven't bought in to all this kumbaya, One World Religion stuff. They realize, as nice as it all *sounds*, that this ecumenical view being perpetrated by Pope Francis, or anyone else, can't be reconciled to biblical **truth**. Christians love unity too, but their unity is in their *love of the truth*, which is found in the Bible, the word of God, and they will not go along with any wind of doctrine just to avoid conflict, to keep or gain friends or followers. For Christians, the word of God is the final word, the standard by which everything else is tested. There are many examples of the Pope's heresies but most shocking: Pope Francis does not ascribe to the non-negotiable doctrine of salvation through Jesus alone. And judging by the words from his own mouth, he is as much a Christian as Satan, himself. He's preaching an "all ways lead to heaven" and an "anything goes" gospel. That sounds a lot like *the broad road that leads to destruction* if you ask me. (Matthew 7:13, Luke 13:24, John 10:7-9). I find it almost shocking that any Christian could fall for this, yet at the same time; I realize that many, even true Christians, those who have accepted Jesus as their Savior but haven't matured in their faith, studied the word of God or prophecy; don't know what the scriptures say about this *subtle* deception. So naturally they assume, surely they can *trust* the Pope; thinking "If we can't trust the Pope, who can we trust?" Especially this one; because he appears to be "such a nice, down to earth guy." Believe me, Satan's counting on that! Although biblical and prophetic scholars may have various insignificant differences that may be up for discussion regarding a variety of topics, one thing true Christians all agree on is this: there is only **One God, One Way and One name** given under heaven where by man must be saved. *Jesus.* That's what seems to rub people the wrong way. Keep in mind, Satan is working over-time and working all the angles in these last days for the purpose of evil and as I said, he's not going down without a fight. But he *is* going down.

Anyway, after the rapture, the people who are left behind will be seduced by, and will succumb to all sorts of demonic deception. I mentioned earlier, the *strong delusion* that will come upon the world in the last days. We're told that it is God Himself who sends the strong delusion at the end of the age. Your first instinct may be to say, "Hey that's not fair." However, before anyone starts complaining about *God sending* a delusion, they should consider the very specific reason He gives for the strong delusion being sent: "The coming of the lawless one is according to the working of Satan, with *all power, signs and lying wonders*, and with all unrighteous *deception* among those who perish, **_because_** they did not receive the love of **the truth** that they might be saved. **_And for this reason_**, God will send them a *strong delusion*, that *they should believe the lie* that they all may be condemned *who **did not** believe the truth* but had pleasure in unrighteousness" (2 Thessalonians 2:9-12).

There is already so much deception in the world today, it's hard to know what Satan could have up his sleeve for the final showdown, but the strong delusion could very likely be the UFO and alien deception that is unfolding before us; and will possibly be in full force at that time. Remember, Jesus called Satan, the father of lies (John 8:44). Meanwhile, many I know personally and love dearly, have fallen into the various carefully set traps of deception and delusion. Satan and his army of demonic spirits are checking off the boxes as they set each trap. Many throughout the world are being deceived as they're being *psychologically conditioned* for the things to come. The apostle, Paul said that Satan, the mystery of lawlessness is already at work. (2 Thessalonians 2:7). And that was way back then; today he's working double-time. People seem to be believing all kinds of things that Satan is doling out, and you don't have to look far to see that he's doling out plenty; he's set up a smorgasbord of *delectable deception*, causing confusion, division, chaos; leading them to seek *unity at the expense of truth*. The wide assortment of deception going on in the world today is merely the shadow of the "strong delusion" that will captivate many. Soon, all may be seeing the *lying signs and wonders* coming from the skies above. "Men's hearts failing them for **fear**, looking after those things which are coming on the earth for the powers of heaven shall be shaken" (Luke 21:26)

When the apostles questioned Jesus about the things to expect at the end of the age, Jesus launched His answer with a stern word of caution: "Do not be deceived." He was very concerned and gave repeated warnings of the *deception* coming upon the world in many forms during the last days. We've been warned that in the last days many will fall away from *the truth* and follow deceptive, evil spirits and doctrines of demons and so forth. The reason for the strong delusion is really pretty simple: The world has been told **the truth** for many years, in many ways, by many people; they have repeatedly rejected **the truth** of God, so He gives them plenty of other things to choose. God's allowing everyone to believe exactly what they want to believe in, whatever it is that makes them *feel* good whatever they *feel comfortable* believing in. God basically says, "You asked for it—you got it." It's that simple. According to the scriptures, it is part of God's judgment for their rejection of **the truth**. We've all heard this expression: "Give them enough rope to hang themselves." It's kind of like that. It is due to mankind's own *rejection of the **truth***, that God turns them over to their own depraved and reprobate minds. The Bible tells us that all mankind has the knowledge of the true God built into them, but they've *deceived themselves*, they've *suppressed the truth*, replacing it with lies that suit their own preferences, lifestyles and evil desires. "They exchanged the truth of God for a lie, and worshiped and served the creature rather than the Creator, who is blessed forever. Amen. *For this reason*, God gave them over to degrading passions; for their women exchanged the *natural* function for that which is unnatural, and in the same way also the men abandoned the *natural* function of the woman and burned in their desire toward one another, men with men, committing indecent acts and receiving in their own persons the due penalty of their error. And just as they did not see fit *to acknowledge God* any longer, God gave them over to a depraved mind, to do those things which are not proper, being filled with *all unrighteousness*, wickedness, greed, evil; full of envy, murder, strife, deceit, malice; they are gossips, slanderers, haters of God, insolent, arrogant, boastful, inventors of evil, disobedient to parents, without understanding, untrustworthy, unloving, unmerciful; and although they know the ordinance of God, that those who practice such things are worthy of death, they not only do the same, but also give *hearty approval* to those who practice them." (Romans 1:25–32). A vivid description of what "enough rope to hang themselves" looks like. All of this describes the world we live in today: a world where men have gone to great lengths to ignore, mock and get rid of all signs of God from the schools to the government. It's not a far stretch to assume this world will have no problem believing in an alien invasion rather than in the living God when the rapture takes place. The point is this: God hasn't changed His mind about what's right and what's wrong, and the truth is that *we all fall short.* There are plenty of offenses to go around and God despises them all: everything from murder and sexual sins to slander and gossiping. We are *all* in need of His forgiveness and grace, and I am no exception to that. For those who choose to reject His grace, God will have the last word on *every* rebellion against Him. At any rate, I continue to pray for the world, for those caught up in the delusion and deception, and to those who give their *hearty approval* to the things that are an offense to God. As long as you still have breath, it's not too late to turn to **the truth** and find forgiveness, and with that, eternal life. Remember the thief on the cross.

Anyway, once this new world leader and his sidekick take over, things will go along "nicely" for a while, but it won't be long till *all hell* will break loose on the planet earth. There is still hope for many, however it will be a horrific time to be alive. We're told during this time—even with the strong delusion, extreme pressure, confusion, and chaos—that the gospel will be preached throughout the world through powerful witnesses appointed by God Himself, and they will lead *many* to **the truth**. Many Jews throughout the Nation of Israel will accept and receive Jesus as their Messiah and be saved in that time as well. Those who refuse to give allegiance to the new leader, who is the antichrist, and refuse the mark that will be required to take part in society during that time, known as the *mark of the beast* will be persecuted, and ultimately they will suffer and die for their faith in Jesus. They are known as *the tribulation saints* and according to the book of Revelation, there will be **many.** They will be *saved into eternal grace* as if snatched from the fire itself, and will be with Jesus for eternity. However, according to scripture, there are no ifs ands or buts when it comes to those who take the mark: they will spend eternity in a horrific place known as hell. Why this hard, fast rule? First of all, those who take the mark, will not be *tricked* into taking it, but will willingly choose to take it. Also, many scholars speculate that the *special mark* that will be required to buy or sell will change or mingle the DNA of its recipients in such a way that they will no longer be redeemable. Much like the circumstances that brought judgement upon the whole earth in the days of Noah, where demons mingled their seed with the women of the earth producing the Nephilim beings: giants and other strange beings which are not fully human but part demon–part human.

(Genesis – 6:1-4). With today's medical, scientific and technological advancements in the area of DNA manipulation, and with Satan at the helm of this sinking ship, anything is possible.

It is debatable among biblical scholars (which I am not) as to whether or not those *who have already heard and rejected* the saving grace of God before the rapture occurs, will be given the opportunity to be saved once the tribulation begins. Although only time will tell, I can't help but think of the many times the scriptures tell us that there's no time like the present. "**Today** is the day of salvation." "Behold, **now** is the acceptable time, behold **now** is the day of salvation." "**Today** if you hear His voice, do not harden your heart" (2 Corinthians 6:2, Psalms 95:7–8, Hebrews 3:15, John 16:8). Those words seem to be a warning: a warning that we don't know what will happen tomorrow, so today is the day to make your choice to be saved for eternity. Also as I read the words "do not harden your heart," they seem to imply that if you hear the truth again and again, and continue to reject it, your heart may become permanently hardened to the truth. The Bible speaks of the continuous rejection of God resulting in the very conscience being seared as with a hot iron so that the heart will no longer be able to distinguish or hear the truth. So it concerns me when people continue to reject the truth of God each time it's offered, because I find it hard to imagine that anyone who is reluctant to live for God today would be willing to die for God later during the tribulation period. There's a good chance they will fall for the strong delusion because of their continuous rejection of God.

I believe that we are living in the last days right now. Although, *the last days* officially began way back in Jesus's time; when I say that I believe that we are living in the last days now, I mean that based on a multitude of evidence, we may very well be the last generation of recorded human history here on earth; Many biblical eschatology scholars agree. There are too many signs to miss if you're looking. But so few are even looking, and many Christians are even being fooled by the deception which is around every corner. There are many signs of the end of the age that are evident in the world today that cannot be said of *any* previous generation. Remember, it was only a little over a hundred-fifty years ago when the first train was all the rage.

Anyway, biblical scholars as well as secular scholars all agree that this generation, unlike any before, has distinct evidence pointing to the end of time rapidly approaching. After World War II, a group of atomic scientists came up with something that they named the Doomsday Clock. It's been monitored and maintained since 1947—a symbol that represents the probability of a man-made global catastrophe, having 12:00 midnight representing what *they* see as the time of the *end of the world*. In January 2020 the Washington Post, CNN, the Independent, and several other major networks and news outlets around the globe reported that the scientist's Doomsday Clock now sits at one hundred seconds till midnight, acknowledging its steady and rapid movement toward *their* expected end of the world. Of course they're trying everything *humanly* possible to slow it down and find a solution for world peace and various other environmental or economic problems not to mention a worldwide virus that subsequently came onto the scene in January 2020 as well. You can Google the Doomsday Clock for more information.

Interestingly enough, the scientist's Doomsday Clock is in lockstep with God's prophetic time clock. In 70 AD the Romans captured the city of Jerusalem and destroyed both the city and the Holy Temple. The Jewish people were without a home and scattered throughout the world for more than two thousand years. Israel was their homeland; it was given to them by God Almighty. The Old Testament prophets not only foretold that the Jews would be scattered out of their land, the prophets Ezekiel and Isaiah foretold that God would bring His people, the Jews, back to their homeland at the *end of the age*. This promise was fulfilled *against all odds* on May 14, 1948. Miraculously too was the prophecy, also now fulfilled, from Zephaniah 3:9 which told of the restoration and revival of their original language of Hebrew, which had been all but lost through the many years of being scattered from their land. The land of Israel had been considered a wasteland for more than a thousand years at that point, but a lot has changed since then. The author Mark Twain confirmed this opinion after his visit to the Holy Land in 1869. To say Twain's reviews were dismal, would be an understatement: "A Hopeless, Dreary, Heart-Broken Land." His observations were in stark contrast to the Israel of today; a land that is flourishing economically, militarily, agriculturally, technologically, and in every way, with the exception of spiritually. Israel today is at the center of our news and current events on a daily basis. No one could have predicted the Jews returning to their homeland, let alone being the *center of attention* of many other surrounding nations; yet God did, and He was right on the money. Since that monumental, unforeseeable event occurred in 1948, the prophetic timepiece of God is ticking; Israel will turn seventy-three years old this year. The prophecies of Isaiah 11:10-12, Isaiah 66:7-8, Ezekiel 36:35, Luke 21:24, Zechariah 12:3:6 have all been fulfilled through the Nation of Israel. As we look at the world today, it's *very likely* that we could be the last generation in God's pre-ordained plan.

It's clear that both biblical scholars and secular scientists, along with the world's top economic strategists, are all watching the world economy at the brink of collapse. Now even more so with a worldwide virus, the extreme weather conditions, the increasing earthquakes and volcanos, the political and civil unrest, wildfires raging, the continuous threat of nuclear weapons, various wars brewing, the increase of lawlessness, and the many other troubling events we're in the midst of. People often respond dismissively to the biblical warning of the end times "wars and rumors of wars, earthquakes," and so on, by saying that these things have always taken place throughout history. However, according to statistics, not only have the occurrences of each of these increased drastically; both in timing as well as intensity, the key is the full convergence of these events in today's world. Everyone from the secular world is desperately trying to figure out what's going on and how to fix it. Everyone (who's looking) is well aware that something ominous and extraordinary is going on in the world today, like at no other time in our history. If you thought that 2020 was rough, buckle up because it's going to get worse. Satan is reveling in his deception, as he sees the world fall into his carefully crafted webs of deceit.

However, Christians—those who are watching—are not surprised about what is going on, and they understand why all these things are happening, understanding all too clearly that this is spiritual warfare in high gear. The world is looking for the answers in the world instead of looking to God's word for the answers. The world's answer to fix everything has always been a One World Government. It goes way back to the Tower of Babel and an arrogant guy named Nimrod; whose very name means rebellious and whose mission was to turn people away from honoring the living God to honoring himself. (Genesis Chapter 10). We all know how things turned out for Nimrod, but as I said, *evil* isn't a quitter. Although this subject of the push towards a One World Government may be considered political, my intention here is to let you know that it happens to be *prophetical* as well. Today, and in fact for many years, a group of elites have followed the Babylonian blueprint: pushing for the one-world solution, using "Chicken Little" cries of global warming now referred to as climate change to infuse fear and bring about what they call "positive change, and *sustainable* solutions" for the world. This power driven, *evil* elite group of Nimrods will stop at nothing, using fear as well as their *moral high ground* to get people to go along with their agenda. And for many it's worked. After all, if you're a "nice person," surely you'll care about your planet for your children and your grandchildren. Right? But anyone who dares to question those propagating the narrative or propose a different perspective, is mocked and spoken of as an intellectual moron who is "denying science" as a means of making them look *ignorant* and even *uncaring*. Many who disagree with their conclusions are scientists themselves! I believe in science as much as anyone, and I also realize that when it comes to "science" there are often differing views on many subjects based on the "expert" you ask; and the subject of "global warming or climate change" is not an exception. Have you ever sat in on or watched a trial on television where each opposing sides bring in their *experts* to prove one point or another? Each expert using verifiable *scientific* methods somehow come up with opposite conclusions. Whether about climate change or any other subject, I find it unsettling when I hear people on the news, or in conversation say, "I'm listening to *the science*." I ask myself, "Who's science?" Because I realize that their message or data may derive from a particular preference, view point or agenda. Many years ago, I remember my sister in law, an oncology nurse, giving her advice of caution and skepticism regarding the *results or findings* of various medical and pharmaceutical studies being done at the time. She cautioned: "Be sure to check to see *who's funding the study* before you come to your conclusion or make **your own** health decision, because there's always an agenda behind each study." That was good advice then and the same principle applies today when it comes to "the science." Science which changes from minute to minute and year to year, and is merely mankind's futile attempt to keep up with God, who created *the science* and Who is the same yesterday, today and forever. The point here is this: there are various "scientific" views on this subject of global warming and climate change as well as the many other subjects that are affecting our world today, and I don't want to spend my time debating them.

However, as a Christian I can say without hesitation that the world has bigger problems than climate change. If you want to talk about climate change and global warming, the Book of Revelation tells us that the entire planet is going to melt with intense heat and be destroyed completely by the wrath of God due to the sin of mankind. Now that's some serious *global warming*! Before that happens, as for viruses, there will be plenty of those as well. In fact according to the scriptures, it will be pestilences ( aka viruses) that will take the lives of a quarter of the earth's population. I'm not telling you any of this to be negative, callus or to scare anyone. But as I said, my purpose in writing this book is to speak *the truth in love*. It wouldn't be very loving of me if I didn't speak the truth about this most serious subject; because I want you to be spared from all of these upcoming events. According to the scriptures, God isn't concerned or displeased about global warming, climate change, the lack of recycling, fossil fuel, carbon footprints, or mankind's "sins against the planet or the environment," or even against each other. But rather God has made clear in His word, that His coming judgment is in direct relation to the sin of **mankind's rejection of Him**, resulting in *rampant immorality and the depravation of mankind*. This ultimate destruction will happen at the end of the tribulation period, and according to all the signs, it is right around the corner. It seems to me that the *globalists and the world* should be less concerned about denying science and more concerned about denying God.

Anyway, this plan for a One World Government is no secret and has been the agenda of the elites and many politicians and world leaders for well over fifty years. This quote from the memoirs of David Rockefeller leaves no room for doubt:

"Some even believe we [the Rockefeller family] are part of a secret cabal working against the best interests of the United States, characterizing my family and me as 'internationalists' and of conspiring with others around the world to build a more integrated global political and economic structure—'One World, if you will.' If that's the charge, I stand guilty and I am proud of it."

On September 11, 1990, amid the Persian Gulf Crisis, George H.W. Bush shared his vision of a New World Order saying in part: "Out of these troubled times, our fifth objective — a new world order can emerge:"

In June of 1990 in a speech at Stanford, Mikhail Gorbachev, former leader of the communist Soviet Union was calling for everyone to work together "for the whole of civilization." saying that "Tolerance is the alpha and omega of a new world order." Several years later regarding the attack on the twin towers, he made an interesting statement: "The victims of the September 11 attack on the United States will not have died in vain if the world leaders *use the crisis* to create a new world order..."

On October 19, 1999, Walter Cronkite accepted the Norman Cousins **Global Governance** Award at a ceremony at the United Nations. The speaker introduced him, saying this: "A one world government is the structure necessary for global justice." Walter Cronkite went on to say: "First, we Americans are going to have to yield up some of our sovereignty. That's going to be a bitter pill. Today, we must develop federal structures on a global level to deal with world problems. We need a system of enforceable world law, a democratic federal world government" Then mocking God, Himself, Cronkite ended his acceptance speech by saying "Join me, I'm glad to sit at the right hand of Satan."

As far back as 1992, then, Delaware Senator, Joe Biden was strongly pushing toward what is commonly referred to as the Globalist system in an article which head-lined a quote from Biden: "How I learned to love the New World Order" He further stated during his Vice Presidency in 2013 "The affirmative task we have now is to create a New World Order." He has been moving swiftly towards this ultimate goal since, and continues his strong push now as our 46th President.

"Come on man," It's not that I don't personally like Joe Biden or any of these other gentlemen. From a worldly perspective, they all *seem* like nice enough guys, but in light of biblical prophecy: knowing that Satan is the force behind this Globalist system and that the Anti-Christ will ultimately be in charge; As a Christian, I'd have to say "Houston, we've got a problem." You don't have to look hard or far to see that the ultimate goal for this group of elites is to bring about a New World Order, a Globalist system as they call it. They're selling it as a noble cause, for the good of everyone. Some in this group may actually believe that. And of course they'll be the ones running it. At least that's what they think. Their ultimate goal is power. Apparently the *perfect world order* that God is planning doesn't suit them. Nimrod wasn't crazy about it either, but God had the last word on Nimrod's big idea. They will all be very surprised when they find out that they've been nothing but puppets, useful idiots for Satan Himself. God is sitting on His throne at this very minute, and you can bet He's laughing, shaking His head at the big idea of the elites, He's saying something like this: "You'll be sorry, your day is coming" (Psalm 2:4, 37: 12, 59:8 ) As you can see the strong push for a One World Government has been going on for a while.

Satan knows how to create a crisis and he knows how to use one to his own advantage! I didn't want to get into this subject because it's become so controversial, but unfortunately it has become like *"the elephant* on the planet" and I believe it relates directly to the coming One World Government and Satan's plan. Conveniently the current pandemic has given an *extra boost* to the globalist agenda. This group of elites realized that their threats of global warming just wasn't get-ting the job done fast enough; they needed more than tree huggers on board. As sinister as this may sound, I believe that the *demonically inspired* powers that be, have *created* the very situation we are in right now for their own evil purpose. I can't stress this enough, "We wrestle not against flesh and blood, but against spiritual forces in dark places..." It's been an experiment, a test of sorts: Those in power are using this virus to see how much control they can gain by propagating *extreme fear,* good old fashioned fear mongering; they know all too well that there is nothing better to use than *fear* to control people. They want to see just how well people will respond in this test and I'm sure they're very pleased with the results.

Shocking to me is how easy it was to manipulate the masses throughout the entire planet in less than a year's time. Think about this reality: the fear of this virus has resulted in *the entire world's compliance:* the world marches in unison, following various rules and mandates; while those in power are making despotic decisions for every individual within their reach based on *the science* of their choosing, according to *their preferred expert*. Meanwhile they're completely bypassing and overriding the long standing legislative steps required to make those decisions–as a dark shadow is cast on the things to come. Of course they tell us that it's for our own good and for the good of everyone else too. Apparently we can't be trusted to make our own health decisions anymore. And to prove you're a nice and caring person, you have to be responsible for the health of everyone else too according to these arbitrary rules. These people have done a real number on society. Between the extreme fear, the passive indifference and the sheer ignorance, many have fallen in line, embraced "the new normal" without any resistance or serious scrutiny; after all, they need to go to the store, the bank, etc. Others simply ignore and dismiss *any* alternative information or opinions, refusing to consider *any* other available data that may contradict or refute the alleged necessity for such mandates. Those who may attempt to explain *any point of view* other than the one widely propagated are quickly, (but rarely quietly) shut down and shut up. They're ostracized, marginalized, called idiots, conspiracy theorists, even accused of being hateful or uncaring about the health of others. Using the term conspiracy theorist on anyone is particularly effective: it's specifically used to shut people down, to smear, shame and ridicule anyone who dares to say anything that doesn't fit the mainstream message. They're immediately *excused* from any "reasonable" conversation.

Anyway, I can truly understand people fearing death if they don't have any eternal security. And I understand generally speaking, as humans, we all have a natural, normal, built-in reasonable sense of self-preservation. But I've had a very difficult time understanding how any Christian can be *so overtaken* by the fear of death that they could fall into this trap, asking myself: "If they truly believe in the living God, then why are they so afraid of losing their life?" It's as if they've forgotten all about Eternal Life! It's as if they've forgotten that it is God who has marked out our days and our times. It's as if they've forgotten all about the promises of God; It's as if they've forgotten all about *the power* that lifted Him from His own grave! The apostle Paul writes about those in the last days who will have a *form of godliness, but deny the power* thereof. (2 Timothy 3:5) During times like this, are God's promises "just a bunch of bible verses" to them? Do they *truly believe* in the *power* of God? I don't know; maybe they just need a reminder. I'm hoping this will refresh them and remind them of Who their God is. Hoping too that they find comfort and courage in *the truth of God's word,* through His Holy Spirit, and that they would be strengthened and encouraged as we face the spiritual battles ahead, because it's going to get rough. Meanwhile, I continue to pray for them all.

As for me: I don't deny that this virus is real, and I don't minimize the seriousness of the virus itself; which is the usual accusation. That's not the case at all. I know people who have had it, and I'm well aware that many have died from it. I also know that people, for as long as they've existed have died from various things, and that everyone is going to die one day, from one thing or another. Those are just the facts of life and I don't take them lightly. That's exactly why I consider *life* so precious. But to me, life means more than just *staying alive.* I also know how to calculate percentages and assess risk factors. I understand and am fully informed as to it's negative, even deadly potential if I happen to get this virus and so on. I also know the power of Satan, the god of this world, who is a master manipulator and the perpetrator of chaos, confusion, division, fear and everything evil. Most importantly, above all, I know the power of God and I trust God. I know that regardless of how bad things get, knowing that they may get a lot worse with talk of a "new strain" on the horizon, God is my anchor. "God has *not* given us the spirit of fear, but of *power,* of *love* and of *a sound mind.*" (2 Timothy 1: 7) My sound mind includes a large dose of common sense. I continue to use basic common sense methods to avoid getting the current virus or any other, but if I happen to get it; "it's not the end of the world" even if I die. I don't live in fear. My common sense also tells me that the things going on in our world today; the *fear,* the *division,* the *death* and *destruction* it's caused, is *not from God.* There's some funny business going on around here, but nobody's laughing. If they are, you won't hear them because they're all *self- quarantining.* My common sense is validated by the word of God. Everything going on *around here* in the world is part of a greater plan and there are bad actors on both sides. And you can be sure Satan doesn't want anyone to hear this message. He loves division, chaos, confusion and fear and he's having a field day with the whole thing. Satan's got most people right where he wants them: People have become so afraid of getting sick or dying from this virus, that they are going to extreme or unusual extents to protect their own life. Or is it their neighbors and others they're protecting? (I'm still confused–who are we protecting again?) They've willingly sacrificed *precious time* with their family, friends, neighbors and loved ones in order to *keep everyone safe*. Sadly to me is that so many people are so afraid of dying or even getting sick, that they've given up on living, both literally and practically speaking. They've willingly traded in warm hugs, friendly smiles and fun-filled gatherings and fellowship for "elbow bumps, masks and drive by or virtual events." As far as I'm concerned, there's nothing social about "social distancing or social media." As I look around, I see everyone seems to be adjusting so well to *the new normal,* that it appears this new world leader won't have much trouble getting people to take his *special mark* when the time comes, they'll be lining up around the corner. They will believe the lie because they refused the love of the truth.

Of the coronavirus pandemic in relationship to the globalist plan, Prince Charles—speaking to his audience at the **World Economic Forum** in March 2020—said this:

"We have a *golden opportunity* to *seize* something good from this crisis -its unprecedented shockwaves may well make people more receptive to big visions of change. As we move from rescue to recover, we have a unique but rapidly shrinking window of opportunity to learn lessons and *reset* ourselves on a more sustainable path. It is an *opportunity* we have never had before and may never have again."

Canadian Prime Minister, Justin Trudeau made this statement:

"This pandemic has provided an *opportunity* for a 'reset.' This is our chance to *accelerate* our pre-pandemic efforts to reimagine economic systems that actually address global challenges like extreme poverty, inequality and climate change."

I mentioned Pope Francis earlier, fitting the bill, or possibly being a mentor for the false prophet of the last days, during the great tribulation; naturally he's also weighed in for the globalist agenda, saying this:

"There is urgent need of a true **world political authority . . . one authoritive source** of oversight and coordination . . . which lays down rules for admissible conduct in light of the **common good**."

Recently commenting on the current pandemic, the Pope said this:

"To come out of this crisis better, we have to recover the knowledge that as a people we have a shared destination. The pandemic has reminded us that no one is saved alone. What ties us to one another is what we commonly call solidarity. Solidarity is more than acts of generosity, important as they are; it is a call to *embrace* the reality that we are bound by bonds of reciprocity. On this foundation we can build a better, different, human future."

The Pope speaks so beautifully and so eloquently but unfortunately his words blatantly contradict the word of God every time he opens his mouth. He's nothing but a smooth talking salesman, selling a deadly bail of goods: He tells us: "we have to *recover the knowledge* that as a people we have a *shared destination.*" Hmmm, Where is he suggesting that we *recover* that knowledge? Apparently he's recovered it from Satan, because it's certainly not from the word of God, which is what he supposedly represents. The knowledge I *recovered* from the scriptures says that we as a people do **not** have a shared destination; rather, it very clearly says there are two very distinct destinations: one is heaven and the other is hell. I'm sure he just doesn't want to *offend* anyone. He goes on to tell us: "no one is saved alone." Really? the bible says that we are each saved alone, one soul at a time, and only through faith in Jesus's death on our behalf. I guess he just forgot to mention Jesus, who said "no man comes to the Father but by me." Then he sums it all up with such hope and optimism: "On this foundation we can build a better, different human future." Oh, it's going to be *different* all right. This Pope has sold his soul to Satan, he's a true wolf in sheep's clothing. I've rarely seen a bigger pile of garbage wrapped up in such a lovely package. "Do not be deceived, beware of wolves in sheep's clothing." He's certainly not going to say "Right this way folks, we're heading to hell."

These are just *a few of hundreds* of quotes from the world's most influential people on the topic of their agenda toward a One World Government. Leaders around the world seem almost giddy, as they proclaim publicly that the Corona virus has given their globalist agenda the *extra boost* they needed to move their plan forward.

If you aren't familiar with scripture, you may be saying, "What's wrong with the idea of globalism and a One World Government? It sounds good to me." However, if you're familiar with scripture, you understand that the problem with the plans of the Rockefellers, the Pope, The Clinton Global Initiative, Klaus Schwab, The World Economic Forum, or any other plans of the elites seeking a *globalist solution* to the world's problems—as nice as they all may *sound*—the globalist plan is the plan of Satan and as I mentioned, it goes way back to the Tower of Babel. In short, the biblical concept is this: God didn't think it was a good idea for any one man, one government or group of elites to have that much power. And God knows best. Many of the things happening today have been foretold thousands of years ago. Christians who know their Bible are not deceived and falling for any of this and they're not living in fear either. They know the outcome of the satanic agenda, and understand that through one means or another, ultimately, **there *will* be a One World Government**; however, they don't jump aboard the global express. They're abiding, using their time and efforts to spread the gospel to as many as possible, until the time when they will no longer be able to, because they will no longer be here. They'll be gone in the twinkling of an eye.

Christians who are tuned in, are looking at what's going on in the world from a biblical perspective; they're examining things through the lens of God's word. They are not living in denial of the *demonic spiritual forces* behind the global agenda. And make no mistake, Satan, the god of this world is working through both sides of this *right-left paradigm* to achieve his ultimate goal of a One World Government. His purpose it to pit people against each other. All this chaos and confusion that we're in the midst of, is spiritual warfare – just another trap Satan has set to cause *division*. And it's working like a *charm*. It's like we're walking through a field of spiritual land mines, strategically placed in every possible area of life, from the churches to the world of politics. That's why it's so important **not** to place your faith or trust in any one man, one leader, one church, one religion, one ideology or any one side, of the *world's system*. Remember, Satan is the ruler of the world's systems. (John 12:31) "He rules the world and has power over everyone who doesn't obey God." (Ephesians 2:2) But test everything, hold everything up to the light of *the word of God*. People are sure to fail you and disappoint you, leaders come and go. However, if you make your choices, cast your votes or take a stand for truth, and the righteousness of God, using *His word* as your measuring rod, you can't go wrong regardless of the outcome. God's word is truth; it will never fail you; it doesn't shift like the winds and the tides; it can't be shaken or moved. Jesus said to His disciples: "Heaven and earth will pass away, but **My word** will not pass away." (Matthew 24:35).

No doubt there are various leaders of this world on both sides from the top down–each playing their part. Who knows? Each may have been especially chosen by Satan for that very role. It doesn't matter– Because God will use them for His glory and for His purpose. There will be many more twists to come in this drama, and the only thing we can count on is the word of God. Like a strategic chess game, God is always one move ahead of Satan. If you are dead set on taking sides, take the side of God. There are many acts and scenes yet to play out in this drama of human history, many events yet to take place coming quickly down the pipe; and many *details* that have *not yet* been revealed to us. As the pieces of the puzzle come together we can only speculate on some of the events that will take place between now and the *final showdown*. But thankfully, God gave us *His word*. Because of that, we know exactly how the story of this world will end. We can be safe with Him during the perilous times ahead: "The heavens will disappear with a roar, the elements will be destroyed by fire, and the earth and all its works will be laid bare." (2 Peter 3:10). In His perfect, preordained time, everything that God has ordained will be revealed and come to pass. Those who place their trust in God, those who take *His side*, will be safe and sound, and will live happily ever after with Him for eternity.

Anyway, we're told in the scriptures that in the end-times, people will replace the truth with a lie and they will worship the creation rather than the Creator. And here we are, with the world doing just that! The warning written thousands of years ago describing the last days of mankind accurately depicting the world we live in today. **"But know this**, that in the last days perilous times will come; For men will be *lovers of themselves*, lovers of money, boasters, proud, blasphemers, disobedient to parents, unthankful, *unholy*, unloving, unforgiving, slanderers, without self-control, brutal, *despisers of good*, traitors, headstrong, haughty, *lovers of pleasure rather than lovers of God*." (2 Timothy 1-4). We shouldn't be surprised; everything is going along exactly according to plan, *exactly* as it has been written. These illusions of grandeur: that mankind is going to save the planet and save humanity is Satan's ruse, he still wants to sit on the throne of the Most High. And although it is Satan's grand plan, God is allowing it to play out and has set a trap of His own for Satan, and for those who choose to follow him. We don't know how each of the *details* will unfold; However, God foretold us some of the things to expect so that we would find comfort and *not be deceived*. Christians today who are acquainted with the scriptures and watching current events are well aware of the days in which we are living. We're watching the stage being set for a One World Government, a One World Leader, and so on. For now, Satan, the god of this world, like the maestro standing before the orchestra is directing it all, everything happening is music to his ears. The World Economic Forum is now calling this plan, "The great reset." Fear is the perfect vehicle to control people and to bring them along. The current "pandemic" and the outbreak of lawlessness throughout the country has given a jump-start to the globalist agenda and has *psychologically conditioned* the world further for things to come.

Now is the time, like no other before, for Christians to realize that we are in the midst of a Holy War – on the battlefield, and our fight is against Satan and his demonic forces. It has never been more important for us to have on the full armor of God: the helmet of *salvation*, the belt of *truth*, the shield of *faith*; and prepare to pick up our *swords*, which is *the word of God*. (Ephesians 6:10-18). It's time for Christians to be sanctifying themselves and taking a stand for *the truth* while they're "watching and waiting for the appearance of their Lord and Savior, Jesus" (Titus 2:11–13, Hebrew 9:27–28, Romans 8:23–25). Not only is that our blessed hope, it is our only hope. I'm not suggesting that Christians should be sitting up on a hillside staring at the sky, but that as they go about their daily business, as they are tuned into current events, they will consider the scriptures in everything, so they won't be fooled or taken by surprise at anything that comes our way. They do not place their trust in men, but in God. They won't be overcome by fear but instead they would be filled with the peace that surpasses all understanding; that they would be trying to share that peace through the gospel with unbelievers at every opportunity. We don't need to worry or be anxious about when our heavenly transport will take place. Jesus tells us this: "But concerning that day and hour, no one knows, not even the angels of heaven" (Matthew 12:32, 24:36). Believers however, have no doubt that it will surely happen. We're told of the signs that point to the end of the age and Jesus's return, and they're everywhere.

Knowing that the rapture will come before the tribulation is a comfort to believers, The scriptures make it clear that we *are not appointed to the wrath* that is fast coming, but will be removed *in the twinkling of an eye* before it begins. And although we don't know when, we are prepared. Jesus's parable of *the ten virgins*, and others explain this concept beautifully. The bottom line is this: "No man knows the day or the hour—but when you see **these things** happening, look up because **your** redemption is near" (Luke 21:28). Today is the day to make your decision for Jesus. And if you already have, then it's time to wake up and smell the coffee. The rapture is imminent and may happen at any time, whether days, months or years I don't know, but we are surely *in the season* of His return. We are seeing these things happening—*these things* that Jesus Himself said to watch for. I want to share this with you now while I have the opportunity so that no one—especially those who I know and love—will be surprised by any of these upcoming events, and *perhaps they'll even listen and be prepared.* As the saying goes: "All I can do is all I can do."

This may sound like some crazy conspiracy or fantasy futuristic stuff I'm talking about here, and I've heard it all. I don't let it bother me and I actually find comfort; because I'm reminded too that the Bible tells us that at the end of the age, in the last days, there will be scoffers who will be mocking the believers who are trying to share this message: many of these mockers are even those calling themselves Christians, the apostate church of the last days–these mockers are actually fulfilling prophecy. And as I said, it doesn't sound so crazy when you consider that the very world we live in today: the technological advancement of DNA manipulation and transhumanism, the robotic and digital society we live in right now; sounded like "crazy, fantasy futuristic stuff" only fifty or so years ago. And I assure you: just as the prophecies, the events of history have up to this point been precisely and accurately fulfilled, everything regarding these future events will take place exactly as it is written. When the last piece of the puzzle is set in its place the picture will become clear. You may doubt now, you may wait till you see for yourself, and when it happens before your eyes, I hope you'll remember this; and I'll pray that it won't be too late.

"Today is the day of your salvation" (2 Corinthians 6:2). As Jesus said to Thomas, "Blessed are those who have not seen, and yet believe" (John 20:29). For believers there is nothing to fear. That's why the Bible refers to the rapture as the blessed hope, telling us to encourage and comfort one another with these words.

Anyway, that was an overview, a condensed, nutshell version of the end-time events, and a detour than I hadn't intended to take when I began this book: but I thought you may be interested in knowing how the story of the world will end as well as some of the things that are rapidly leading up to that day. I'll continue to pray that you'll be on the *winning side* when it does. My primary purpose for this book is to share the gospel with you: to let you know that God loves you, He sent His only begotten Son, Jesus to die for your sins, and that you can have eternal life through faith in His sacrifice on your behalf. If you have an interest to know more about prophecy, there are lots of books and information available about the various prophetical *signs of the times* in relation to current events. I would suggest you go to the scholars of eschatology and biblical prophecy for more in-depth information.

These are some of many verses throughout scripture regarding the rapture of the Church and the events of the end times:

"As it was in the days of Noah, **so it will be at the coming of Jesus, the Son of Man.** For in the days before the flood, people were eating and drinking and marrying and giving in marriage, up to the day Noah entered the ark. . . . That is how it will be at the coming of the Son of Man. Two men will be in the field; one will be taken and the other left. Two women will be grinding with a hand mill; one will be taken and the other left. Therefore, **keep watch, because you do not know on what day your Lord will come.**" (Matthew 24:42)

"For **you know** very well that **the day of the Lord will come** like a thief in the night. For when **they say,** 'Peace and safety!' then suddenly destruction comes upon **them,** as labor pains upon a pregnant woman. **And they** shall *not* escape. **But you,** brethren, are not in darkness, so that this Day should overtake you as a thief. **You** are the sons of light and sons of the day. **We** are not of the night nor of darkness. Therefore **let us** not sleep, as others do but **let us** watch and be sober. For those who sleep, sleep in the night, and those who get drunk are drunk at night. But **let us** who are of the day be sober, putting on the breastplate of faith and love, and as a helmet, the hope of salvation. For God **did not appoint us to wrath, but to obtain salvation** through our Lord Jesus Christ, who died for us, that whether we wake or sleep, **we** should live together with Him. Therefore, comfort each other and edify one another." (1 Thessalonians 5:2–11)

"Immediately after the distress of those days, "the sun will be darkened and the moon will not give its light; the stars will fall from the sky, and the heavenly bodies will be shaken" (Matthew 24:29).

"But the day of the Lord **will come like a thief.** The heavens will disappear with a roar; the elements will be destroyed by fire, and the earth and everything in it **will be laid bare**" (2 Peter 3:10).

"Tell us if You are the Christ, the Son of the Living God! Jesus said to him, '**It is as you said.** Nevertheless, I say to you hereafter you will see Me sitting at the right hand of the Power, **and coming on the clouds of heaven**'"(Matthew 26:63–64).

"Brothers and sisters, we do not want you to be uninformed about **those who sleep in death,** so that you do not grieve like the rest of mankind, **who have no hope.** For we believe that **Jesus died and rose again**, and so we believe that God will bring with Jesus those who have fallen asleep **in Him.** According to the Lord's word, we tell you that we who are still alive, who are left until the coming of the Lord, will certainly not precede those who have fallen asleep. For the Lord Himself will come down from heaven, with a loud command, with the voice of the archangel and with the trumpet call of God, and **the dead in Christ will rise first.** After that, **those who are still alive** and are left **will be caught up together** with them in the clouds **to meet the Lord in the air.** And so we will be with the Lord forever. Therefore **encourage one another with these words.**" (1 Thessalonians 4:13–18)

"I declare to you, brothers and sisters, that flesh and blood cannot inherit the kingdom of God, nor does the perishable inherit the imperishable. Listen, I tell you a mystery: **We will not all sleep, but we will all be changed in a flash,** in *the twinkling of an eye,* at the last trumpet. For the trumpet will sound, the dead will be raised imperishable and those who remain will be changed." (1 Corinthians 15:50–52)

"But someone may ask, 'How will the dead be raised? What kind of bodies will they have?' What a foolish question! When you put a seed into the ground, it doesn't grow into a plant unless it dies first. And what you put in the ground is not the plant that will grow, but only a bare seed of wheat or whatever you are planting. Then God gives it the new body He wants it to have. A different plant grows from each kind of seed. Similarly there are different kinds of flesh—one kind for humans, another for animals, another for birds. And another for fish. There are also bodies in the heavens and bodies on the earth. The glory of the heavenly bodies is different from the glory of the earthly bodies. The sun has one kind of glory, while the moon and stars each have another kind. And even the stars differ from each other in their glory. It is the same way with the resurrection of the dead. Our earthly bodies are planted in the ground when we die, but **they will be raised to live forever**. Our bodies are **buried in brokenness**, but they will be **raised in glory**. They are **buried in weakness**, but they will be **raised in strength**. They are **buried as natural human bodies**, but they will be **raised as spiritual bodies.** For just as there are natural bodies, there are also spiritual bodies." (1 Corinthians 15:35–42)

"Jesus said 'Do not let your hearts be troubled. You believe in God; believe also in me. My Father's house has many mansions; if that were not so, I would not have told you that I am going there to prepare a place for you. And if I go and prepare a place for you, **I will come back and take you to be with me** that you also may be where I am'"(John 14:1–3).

"But Christ has indeed been raised from the dead, the first fruits of those who have fallen asleep. For since **death came through a man, the resurrection of the dead comes also through a man**. For as **in Adam all die**, so **in Christ all will be made alive**. But each in turn: Christ, the first fruits; then, **when He comes**, those who **belong to Him**." (1 Corinthians 15:20–23)

"Jesus said to her, 'I am the resurrection and the life. The one who believes in me will live, even though they die; and whoever lives and believes in me will never die. Do you believe this?' (John 11:25-26)

"At that time Michael, the great prince who protects your people, will arise. There will be a time of distress such as has not happened from the beginning of nations until then. But at that time **your people—**everyone **whose name is found written in the book of life will be delivered.** The multitudes **who sleep in the dust of the earth will awake**: some to everlasting life, others to shame and everlasting contempt." (Daniel 12:1–2)

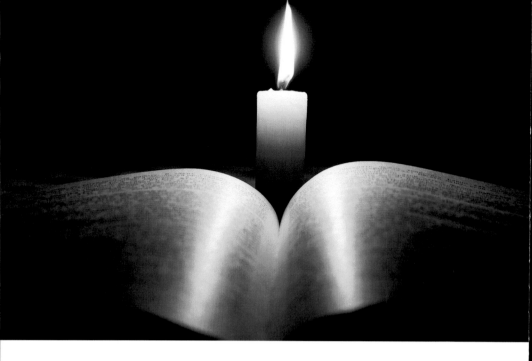

"How will we escape if we neglect so great a salvation?
After it was at first spoken through the Lord,
it was confirmed to us by those who heard. "(Hebrews 2:3)

## *Chapter Thirty-Two*

## WHY ME LORD?

S ome of these things that I've shared with you here may be things you've never heard before; they may even come as a shock or a surprise. But I assure you that every word of scripture will be fulfilled exactly as it is written. More likely there are many things that I've shared within these pages that may be things you've heard all of your life. You may have been raised in a family where you heard some of the well-known stories from the Bible, or maybe you went to a church as a child where you learned some biblical truths, as I had. You may have heard about Adam and Eve and the forbidden fruit, Noah's ark and the great flood. You may even have heard that Jesus died for your sins and rose again on the third day, that Jesus is the Savior of the world, and so on; you may have celebrated Christmas and Easter, but you never really gave any of it much thought or consideration; you never took it to heart, you never understood what it all meant, and you never realized that there was a choice for you to make, or the gravity of that choice.

Being raised in the Catholic Church, that was the case with me. Being Catholic was just something that I was, like being Irish. Like many who have been raised going to church each Sunday, whether Catholic, Presbyterian, Lutheran, Methodist, or whatever, I had heard all of those things and more. Although I can only speak from my own Catholic experience, I can say that I was never taught throughout all my years of catechism classes that the one and only requirement for salvation is **faith** in the *finished* work of Jesus. There was no talk about having a personal relationship with God the Father through His Son, Jesus, or the indwelling of the Holy Spirit. In the Catholic Church, I was encouraged to receive various sacraments, to follow church and moral rules, to confess my sins to a priest weekly, idolatry was encouraged in every area: encouraging prayers and worship to the Virgin Mary and various saints, praying on rosary beads, and so on. From what I could gather, all this was done as the means to secure my salvation and receive forgiveness, with the hope of getting to heaven. But at the same time, the Catholic Church kept the threat of burning in hell very real if you weren't good enough. If you weren't too bad, there were a couple of "in between" places called Limbo and Purgatory that you may end up in too, for one reason or another after you died; you'd have to hang out there until other people have prayed enough, or lit enough candles to get you into heaven. I didn't understand it all, but we were just going through the motions of *being Catholic*. At home we were just taught to be nice and to "behave."

It wasn't till I read the Bible years later that I not only saw the many and glaring contradictions of what I had been taught throughout my years of Catholic teachings but realized that there were what seemed to me, some pretty important omissions. I am not making a blanket statement about *all* Catholics, because I do believe that some in the Catholic Church **may** find salvation through faith in Jesus. But I'd have to say, it seems it would be purely by accident rather than by design. As I look back at this now, I see that all of these things—the rituals, the penance, the sacraments—were diversions and distractions that led me away from grace and, more than that, diminished the sacrifice of Jesus, which was all I really needed in the first place.

Anyway, it wasn't till I was about twenty-six years old that I picked up a Bible for the first time. My son Peter was at a sleepover, my husband was out with some friends, and I was alone that night. I was all settled in to watch my favorite show at the time, *Hart to Hart*, when the power in my area suddenly went out due to an electrical storm. Although we had just moved in, thankfully I had a box of candles up in my cupboard. Earlier that day my sister, Sue, had come by to visit and she brought me a housewarming gift. **It was a Bible.** I wasn't really a Bible-reading kind of girl, and I definitely wasn't interested in being called a "Jesus freak." But it was so typically thoughtful of my sister, so I graciously thanked her and I put it up on the shelf in my living room. I hadn't finished unpacking from our move, so the book from my sister was the only thing on my shelf at the time. I really never expected to read it, but it seems that God had different plans, and that night out of sheer boredom, due to a power outage, I opened up my new Bible to **the Book of Romans.** As I began reading, I experienced something that to this day I can't quite explain, other than to say it was a mystery, a miracle of sorts, something I **never** could have imagined happening to me took place; I was profoundly moved by the Holy Spirit of God. The electrical power was out, but as I sat there reading in near-darkness, thankfully the power of God was not. It was illuminating brightly, as if someone had flipped a switch, and I knew without a doubt that what I was reading was directly from God, the very God who I had heard about my whole life, yet a God who I never **knew** till that night. He was speaking directly to my heart, and I recognized my own need for a savior in that very moment as the words jumped out at me: "There is none righteous, no, not one." (Romans 3:10). "All have sinned and fallen short of the glory of God" (Romans 3:23). I instantly knew I was included in that word *all*. Reading on, "The wages of sin is death, but the **gift** of God is eternal life in Jesus Christ our Lord" (Romans 6:23). I understood the sacrifice that Jesus made for me. I knew it was personal. I continued to read, and as foreign and strange as the words seemed to be, the simple, clear message of the gospel had reached my heart. Just like that! There were no lightning bolts, no roaring thunder, no harps or trumpets sounding, no angels singing. There wasn't a heavenly glow surrounding me; it was as simple as a quiet acknowledgement in my mind, and my heart had changed, and in fact *my entire perspective* about nearly everything changed that night, in an instant. Since then over the course of many years, I have come to better understand the depth and enormity of His sacrifice.

I often hear of dramatic stories of God changing people's lives very drastically; literally from the grips of death or addiction or other places we might call rock-bottom. My experience was hardly dramatic, but had a very profound effect. Back then, like most people my age, my life wasn't perfect, but from a worldly standpoint, it was pretty darn close: I was young and healthy, I was married and pregnant with my second child, I was a stay-at-home mom, and we had just moved into a cute little condo. At that point in my life, as a single teen mom in the '70s, I had already fought my way out of rock-bottom places, weathered many personal storms, and my life seemed to be heading for sunny skies. By all *outward* appearances, I had it all together. Yet with all that, although no one would have known, *inwardly*, I always felt an emptiness; a deep sadness that I couldn't explain or shake. Generally speaking, being more of a listener than a talker, I didn't talk about my feelings much; assuming other people may feel the same way too. So I continued on, conscientious and deliberate in maintaining an upbeat *exterior* demeanor. However, no matter what I had accumulated or accomplished, there remained a sense that something was missing, but I couldn't put my finger on it.

That feeling is the very essence of the human condition. We are all trying to fill a void: a void that can only be filled by God. We continue the pursuit, only to find that possessions, positions and even people will fail you at times. But that's just what we humans do: we have our *goals*, we keep placing *that* one more *thing* in our sights, assuming each time, it will be the one thing that will fill the void. Without God, mankind will continue this quest, until their time is up, only to realize that Jesus was right: "For what shall it profit a man, if he should gain the whole world, but lose his soul?" (Mark 8:36)

That night I found what was missing from my life: It was God—and although I didn't even know it at that time, it was **truth** that I sought. Deep within every heart is a yearning for **truth.** I knew that night, without *any* doubt, that I had found the One, true *living God*. It was like finding the instruction booklet for life from the very giver of life, written into a love letter from Him. I remember as a very little girl, laying down on the grass looking up at the sky, and wondering about God; was He watching me, was He listening to me, did He know me? That night I knew the answers to all of those questions. Not only were the answers "YES," I knew right then that I was *loved by Him*. And finally, that night, I had the truth set before me, piercing my heart with such intensity; it was a sense of joy and relief; like I had found something that I had lost, something that I had been looking for, for a very long time.

Even as I sat there in my "cute little condo," it felt as though God had pulled me out of the trenches. As the years have passed, the more I realize that He did just that, and has done it in various ways and times since, throughout my life. He filled the hole in my heart that nothing in the world could ever have filled. I understood the purpose of life and was filled with a sense of completeness, joy, and peace. Although I didn't understand all the ramifications of what had happened that night, and I can't give adequate words to explain the miraculous work of God that took place, I can say that literally and instantly I had a new song in my heart—I had a hunger to know more about God, and I continued to read and study. I could barely contain my excitement. I knew that I had found the truth and I wanted to share it. It was what you would call nowadays an "'ah-ha' moment"! Although it was greeted with ridicule, opposition, and indifference for the most part.

I remember the night that I understood and accepted God's grace, nearly forty years ago. It was as if a weight had been lifted from my soul in an instant; I was instantly infused with joy and excitement. My external transformation may not have been evident at times in some of the years that followed, as I struggled with strong opposition and the forces of the world around me, and my own nature and free will, but the internal, spiritual transformation was instantaneous, miraculous, and life-changing. It was as if a veil of darkness had been removed and I could see for the very first time. I knew the truth was in the Bible, and I have never doubted it for a moment since. I thought of the words of John Newton's beloved song "**A**mazing **G**race": "I once was blind but now I see." At that moment I understood what he meant when he wrote those words. And to this day, the change that took place in that moment is still a mystery to me, and I consider it nothing less than a miracle.

Thinking back: In my initial excitement of finding the truth within the pages of the bible, I wanted to share this good news with everyone I knew so that they could be saved too, I wanted to be a light in the world, and so on. Finally understanding *the grace of God*, I didn't want to appear "legalistic" about my faith. My husband at that time wasn't a believer, and the few Christians I knew back then didn't seem to share in my extreme excitement and zeal. They had a kind of *casual* attitude towards Christianity, and would quote out of context, classic verses "judge not lest you be judged..." and saying "Remember, Jesus hung out with tax collectors and sinners..." As if to say, "Jesus is 'cool' with whatever..." so I found myself trying to *fit in* rather than trying to *stand out*. For new believers, I would encourage you to remember this: Yes, Jesus did spend time talking to the tax collectors and sinners, but Jesus directly confronted them with **the truth** and He called them to **repentance**; He isn't 'cool' with whatever, and His example shows that it wasn't Jesus's goal to *fit in* with the world, but rather to bring them *out* of the world. Those that Jesus *hung out with*, were made new creations spiritually, upon their encounter with Him; in other words, they had already been *transformed by Him*, before He "hung out" with them. As a new Christian, like many others, I had it backwards. I was blending in rather than setting myself apart, only to find that trying to lead anyone to Christ by doing this was utter foolishness; it can open the door for Satan to slip in, and will leave you in a continuous spiritual struggle with the very Spirit of God. I spent many wasted years in that condition as my spiritual growth waivered: trying to navigate my way through the darkness of the world, failing miserably and grievously at times, and I was hardly a worthy ambassador for a Holy God; still through all of that, I never lost sight of *the truth*.

What I understand to be a spiritual birth occurred that night nearly forty years ago, as I believed *the truth* in the words I was reading. They say hindsight is twenty-twenty. The lessons I've learned along the way are these: if you try to fit in, you'll find that's all you will do, "fit in" and you may even "fall in." Most importantly, you won't make a difference for God. The less time you spend *in the word*, the more lost you'll become *in the world*. One of my favorite pastors from a church I attended many years ago used to say something like this: "In the world you can *rationalize* just about anything. On the other hand, when you're in the **word**, there's no way around the truth." *Feelings, emotions* and *circumstances* change from minute to minute, but the truth remains the same. So if you stay firmly anchored in truth, you will stay on course. Anyway, I thank God every day for my sister, Sue, who brought me that Bible. She told me later, that after she dropped it off, she was praying for me on her way home, praying that God would prepare my heart to hear His voice. Well, her prayers were answered, as I heard His voice loud and clear that night, and I couldn't help but **believe**.

Why me? I don't know the answer to that, but I'm thankful and in awe, every time I think of the grace of God and the fact that He saved me. I don't know why I heard and believed and why others don't. That remains somewhat of a mystery to me, because I can't see into the hearts of others, but God can. Maybe the answer can be explained by the parable Jesus told about *the sower and the soil.* (Matthew 13:1-23) I don't know for sure, but I know that there is nothing special about me, nothing particularly good, and I'm certainly no better than anyone else. But for some reason, that night I heard and I believed. Why did my belief result in an instant change of heart toward God? I don't know, but I always remember that Satan *"believes"* in God too. So I understand that it is more than an intellectual belief that leads to salvation. The apostle, John tells us this: "If you confess with your mouth that Jesus is Lord, and *believe in your heart* that God raised Him from the dead, you will be saved. For it is **with your *heart* that you *believe* and are justified** and it is with your *mouth* that you *profess* **and are saved.**" (John 14:1) God works through His people, and **His word** is like a double-edged sword, cutting both ways to those who hear it: the truth will either excuse or accuse, and ultimately it will bring either life or death based on the condition and desire of each heart it reaches. "For the word of God is alive and exerts power, and is sharper than any two-edged sword, piercing through, even dividing the soul and spirit, and of the joints and their marrow, and is able to discern the thoughts and intentions of the *heart*" (Hebrews 4:12). As I mentioned earlier, I believe every heart has a deep yearning to know the truth. However, once found, each will respond to it in one of two ways:

they will either *embrace it* or they will *dismiss it and possibly despise it*. I think of two children, each given a gift that was especially chosen for them by someone who knows their every *need* and who loves them very much. The children *can't wait* to open their gifts. However, when they finally do, one child will toss it to the side with no sign of appreciation, perhaps even anger in their disappointment, and the other child will clutch it to his or her chest and say with joy and excitement, "Thank you! It's just what I've always wanted."

Why me? I don't know, but through the scriptures, we know this much is certain: "God gives grace to the humble and He resists the proud" (1 Peter 5:5). I think of Neil Young's song "Heart of Gold" or Bruce Springsteen singing "Hungry Heart." As far as I can tell, God is simply looking for a humble heart, a heart that recognizes that they are lost without Him. Even with that, we can't take any credit, because without God calling us to Himself, without His offering us the gift of salvation and eternal life, and ultimately, without the work of His Holy Spirit, we would still be *guilty, helpless and hopeless*. So I am ever thankful. "It's just what I've always wanted!" My life has taken many twists and turns and many ups and downs, and I've found myself wandering in the world like a prodigal child during periods of time on my journey from then till now. But God has been faithful, and His Holy Spirit drew me back each time, holding nothing against me; With the compass out of my pocket now, He gently corrects me and points me in the right direction, and He continues to carry me through each trial I face. That's God's grace, and there's nothing else that compares to it. It brings the peace that surpasses all understanding. Because of Him, my heart is filled with joy and continues to sing a new song every day, even through the muck and mire that come with life. I'm sticking close to Jesus and appreciate Him now more than ever before, as we approach the end of the age, the end of the world as we know it.

"Enter through the narrow gate. For wide is the gate and broad is the road that leads to destruction, and many enter through it. But small is the gate and **narrow the road** that leads to life, and only a few find it."
(Matthew 7:13-14)

## Chapter Thirty-Three

## BUT WHAT ABOUT YOU?

In closing, I return to the one thing we can all relate to: the reality of death. It's the simple but harsh reminder that our days here on this earth are numbered. The finality of death is the hardest part to bear, and although the pain lingers, God's promises give me strength, comfort, and hope—not only in my present life but even when I face death, knowing without a doubt that I will be instantly in God's presence for eternity. God's offer is a "lifetime offer," but His offer *expires* when we

164

do. My intent is not to judge you or to scare you but to offer you **truth**; because *only in truth*, is there hope; the kind of hope that means to greatly anticipate, without doubt, the things that God has promised. We can have full assurance because Jesus, the very Son of the Eternal God, defeated death. This is not a message of doom and gloom or that the sky is falling, and I'm not trying to rain on anyone's parade; I'm not telling you that the world is going to end today, tomorrow, next month or next year. Whether you believe in the rapture or the great tribulation or not, one thing we all believe in and *know* is this: our life here on earth can end at any moment; we are all one heartbeat away from death. The apostle James put it like this: "You do not know what tomorrow will bring. What is your life? For you are but a mist, a vapor that appears for a little time then vanishes"(James 4:14). Death is the reality we all face every day, and it is within that reality, that truth, where we find hope from the word of the Living God, which has been recorded and preserved for us. That ultimate and final reality of death brings understanding and points us to eternity. This was written by King Solomon, considered by many to be the wisest man ever to have existed: "It is **better** to go to a house of mourning than to go to a house of feasting, for death is the destiny of everyone; the living should take this to heart" (Ecclesiastes 7:2). The Psalmist tells us this: "Teach us to number our days that we may gain a heart of wisdom" (Psalms 90:12).

This message may come to you as a wake-up call as you consider these things regarding your own eternity, as you examine your own life and mortality, and as you see the confusion and uncertainty of the world we live in. I wanted to carefully and thoughtfully explain my position in the best way I can, to offer you this important food for thought, "to give an account for the hope that is in me," (1 Peter 3:15) and most of all, to plead my case to you for **Jesus;** He is our only hope, as He proclaimed: "I am The *way*, The *truth* and The *life*. **No man** comes to the Father **but by Me**" (John 14:1–14). In this world there are many ways you can go, but only *one way* that leads to the Father, who is in heaven. In this world, deception and lies about what happens when we die are abundant, but there is only *one truth*. In this world we may have life for a short time, but only through Jesus do we have *eternal life*. The apostle Matthew tells us, "Enter through the **narrow gate**. For wide is the gate and broad is the road that leads to destruction, and many will enter through it. But small is the gate and narrow the road that leads to life, and only a few find it." (Matthew 7:13-14)

The ending of the story of the world we live in, and all those who will enter into eternal life, is already known to God. He's already watched from beginning to end, the entire, epic drama of mankind; He's got what I like to call, the **DVD** so to speak: the **Divine View** of **Destiny.** However, each act and scene will continue to play out for us until the *appointed* time of His return. Considering all of your options, my prayer is that you'll consider Jesus, consider the recorded evidence of His divine nature, as God in the flesh, and consider His offer: the amazing gift of eternal life that He has paid for with His own life. Consider all of these things that I have shared with you about the gift of God's precious grace, and consider the alternatives. I echo the conclusion of Pascal: "It's your best bet."

As you consider these things, I will be praying that through faith you'll enter through the narrow gate that leads to life. Jesus loves you so much that He shed His own blood and died on the cross for **your** sins. There is no greater love than this, and He is waiting for you to come to Him that you may have eternal life. "There is no other name given under heaven where by man **must** be saved" (Acts 4:12). Everyone has faith in something, and everyone—regardless of what they believe—will come face-to-face with **the truth** as they make their own *discovery* one day about what will happen when they die. When all is said and done, it will not be "my truth" or "your truth" that will count, it will be *the truth*: the truth of the *one*, *true* and *only* Almighty God. And although I realize that everyone can't be right, I also accept that everyone has the right and the free will to choose what they will believe, where, what or in whom, they will place their faith. As for me, I can say with confidence, "I know in Whom I have believed" (2 Timothy 1:12).

As for all of us, as for today and our time here before the **truth** is revealed to each of us, regardless of your choice, or where you *believe* you'll spend eternity or whatever or whomever your faith may be in, one thing I hope we can all agree on is this: while we're here on earth for this brief time, we should love one another. No matter what your decision, I love you. I love you enough to tell you the **truth**, and I'll continue to pray for you. Death is a reminder that our life here is short and fleeting at best. It reminds us to be more patient and kinder to each other, because after all, "nobody's perfect." It reminds us that the last time you see someone, those last words spoken may be *just that*—**the last**.

Death is the *not-so-subtle* reminder that our life here is precious, fragile, and unpredictable, for sure. Our time here on this earth is merely a speck on the canvas of eternity. Today, while I'm still here, I wanted to offer you this message of hope, a light at the end of the tunnel we call life, and a light to guide your steps as you go through it: Jesus, the light of the world, who said, "Whoever follows Me will never walk in darkness, but will have the light of life." Meanwhile I'll be praying that I see you in heaven. Why go anywhere else? Everything boils down to one thing: *Jesus*. As for now, this is the question for you to contemplate; it's the question that Jesus asked His own disciples: "But what about you? Who do you say that I am?" (Matthew 16:15).

With Love, Nancy

*N*ancy Hollywood-Leamer was born in McKeesport, Pennsylvania on November 20*ᵗʰ* 1955 to Joseph and Virginia Hollywood. In 1964 the Hollywood family moved to Granada Hills, California, in the heart of the San Fernando Valley. She grew up there, in "the Valley," as they fondly referred to it, along with her five brothers, Tim, Jack, Jimmy, Robert and Patrick, and her three sisters, Jan, Sue and Lynn. Today she's happily married and living with her husband, Gregg, in Llano, California.

She has seven children and twelve grandchildren and she loves them all. She's suffered many tragic and untimely losses throughout her lifetime; including the loss of four of her siblings, her first husband, and most devastating, her beloved daughter, Nichol. Through her faith and personal tragedies, she shines a light at the end of the tunnel, which is Jesus, who said "I am the light of the world, whoever walks with me will **never walk in darkness**; but have the light of life" He also proclaims, "I am the resurrection and the life. **Whoever believes** in me, will live, even though they die." (John 11:25, John 8:12)

*"What is your life? You are but a mist that*
*appears for a little while and then vanishes." (James 4:14)*

*Back row: my sister, Sue, our Mom, holding youngest brother, Patrick, my sister, Jan- Front row: my brother, Jack, my sister, Lynn, my brother, Jimmy, me and my brother, Robert –*
*Granada Hills 1966*

*My first son, Peter – 1974*

*Me with my first daughter, Nichol -1982*

*My Dad and my five brothers, Jimmy, Patrick, Jack, Robert and Tim -1986*

*Jason, Ally, Rachel and Nichol -1991*

*Nichol, Ally, Rachel and Jimmy – 1992*

*Me and my dear friend, Julie- 1997*

*Me, my younger sister, Lynn and our Mom –*
*Annual Mother's Day Celebration–2008*

*Our Mom's 85<sup>th</sup> Birthday–family, friends and neighbors came to celebrate -2013*

*My dear friend Karen -2016*

*My Mom with my dear friend Renee-2018*

*My dear friends Patti, Erin and Laurie- 2018*

*My dear friend, Chris- 2020*

*Back row: my nephew, Danny, me, Lindsay and their daughter, Piper, next row-*
*Brother-in-law, Steve, my sister, Sue, my Mom, my niece, Tracie and Danny and*
*Lindsay's other daughter, Charlotte*
*At my Mom's house–2018*

*Our last family Christmas with my Mom at our house in Llano, 2018
Top- Jimmy, granddaughter, Angel, next row- my husband Gregg's son, Travis, Gregg,
my daughter, Ally, my grandson, Nico, my Mom, Me, my grandson, Zayn, next
row- Eddie, daughter-in-law, "T", Son in law, Jeremy, my granddaughter, Sun, my
daughter, Breezy, my daughter, Rachel, granddaughter, Janie, my oldest Son Peter
and my daughter-in- law, Elisa*

*Family Christmas at our house in Llano, 2019-*
*Gregg, Jimmy, Elisa, Tononzin, Ozge, Hannah, me, Janie, Ally, Nico, Rachel, Zayn,*
*Jeremy, and Peter*

*My daughter, Nichol, my oldest son, Peter, me and my daughter-in-law, Elisa–2010*

*My daughter, Nichol- 2014*

*My daughter, Rachel- 2017*

*My daughter, Ally, my grandson, Nico, and me - 2018*

*My son, Jimmy, his wife, Tononzin, my Mom, me and my Husband, Gregg 2017*

*My youngest daughter, Breezy - 2019*

*My Grandaughter, Jazzy -2019*

*Grandaughters, Evalina and Sunny in front of church- 2019*

*Grandaughter, Janie in front of the church Christmas tree- 2019*

*My grandson, Zayn -2018*

*My newest grandson, "Baby Carter" 2020*

*Six of my twelve grandchildren–Evalina, Sunny,*
*Zayn, Baby Carter, Nico and Jane 2020*

*Gregg and me 2009*            *Gregg and me 2019*

*"Teach us to number our days that we may gain a heart of wisdom."*
*(Psalm 90:12)*